RESEARCH REPORT   FEBRUARY 2013

Turning Around Low-Performing Schools in Chicago

University of Chicago Consortium on Chicago School Research: *Marisa de la Torre, Elaine Allensworth, Sanja Jagesic, James Sebastian, and Michael Salmonowicz* **American Institutes for Research:** *Coby Meyers and R. Dean Gerdeman*

TABLE OF CONTENTS

1 Executive Summary

5 Introduction

Chapter 1
9 Chicago's School Reform Efforts

Chapter 2
17 Students in the Schools after Intervention

Chapter 3
31 Teachers in the Schools after Intervention

Chapter 4
37 Student Outcomes in the Schools after Intervention

Chapter 5
47 Interpretive Summary

53 References

55 Appendix

89 Endnotes

Acknowledgements

The authors would like to recognize the many people who helped make this study possible. Our colleagues at the University of Chicago Consortium on Chicago School Research, REL Midwest, and American Institutes for Research (AIR) gave critical feedback and supported us at each stage of this project. We are also very grateful for the critical review and feedback we received from the anonymous reviewers as part of the original contract from IES to do this work. We are indebted to members of the Steering Committee and others who provided substantive feedback on our research. Don Fraynd, Reyna Hernandez, and Lynn Cherkasky-Davis, as well as Rebecca Herman and Johannes Bos from AIR all performed careful reviews of this manuscript. CCSR directors Melissa Roderick, Sue Sporte, and Jenny Nagaoka each provided us with thoughtful comments on this report. Emily Krone, CCSR Director for Outreach and Communications and Bronwyn McDaniel, CCSR Communications and Research Manager, were instrumental in helping us edit and produce this report. Eliza Moeller and Kaleen Healey performed a very thorough technical read on the final draft. Our work would not have been possible without student records provided by Chicago Public Schools.

This work was supported in part under U.S. Department of Education Institute of Education Sciences (IES) contract ED-06-CO-0019 by Regional Educational Laboratory Midwest; it was administered by Learning Point Associates, an affiliate of AIR. The content does not necessarily reflect the views or policies of IES or the U.S. Department of Education nor does mention of trade names, commercial products, or organizations imply endorsement by the U.S. government. This report also benefited from funding to CCSR from the Spencer Foundation, which supports research for the improvement of education.

This report was produced by UChicago CCSR's publications and communications staff: Emily Krone, Director for Outreach and Communications; Bronwyn McDaniel, Communications and Research Manager; and Jessica Puller, Communications Specialist.

Graphic Design: Jeff Hall Design
Photography: David Schalliol and Cynthia Howe
Editing: Ann Lindner

2.2013/pdf/jh.design@rcn.com

Executive Summary

In recent years, the nation's lowest-performing schools have increasingly become a focal point of scrutiny and concern. Policymakers have called for swift and dramatic action to improve the nation's 5,000 lowest-performing schools, arguing that the magnitude of their dysfunction requires a robust response.

Specific strategies for "turning around" chronically low-performing schools have become prominent, with the U.S. Department of Education enacting policies to promote four school improvement models that include "fundamental, comprehensive changes in leadership, staffing, and governance."[1] Spurred by federal grants and incentive programs, states and districts are attempting to catalyze rapid improvement in the lowest-performing schools through efforts such as replacing principals, firing every member of the staff, and closing schools entirely.

Despite the attention and activity surrounding these types of school improvement models, there is a lack of research on whether or how they work. To date, most evidence has been anecdotal, as policymakers have highlighted specific schools that have made significant test score gains as exemplars of school turnaround, and researchers have focused on case studies of particular schools that have undergone one of these models. This has led to a tremendous amount of speculation over whether these isolated examples are, in fact, representative of turnaround efforts overall—in terms of the way they were implemented, the improvements they showed in student outcomes, and whether these schools actually served the same students before and after reform.

To begin addressing this knowledge gap, the University of Chicago Consortium on Chicago School Research and American Institutes for Research (AIR) partnered to examine five different models initiated by the Chicago Public Schools (CPS) in 36 schools. CPS was an early adopter of dramatic intervention strategies in low-performing schools, and the reforms in this study were implemented between 1997 and 2010, before the federal government released its recommendations for turning around chronically low-performing schools. All of the schools were identified as chronically low performing by the district and were reformed in ways consistent with the elements described in the school improvement models recommended by the federal government, despite differences in the names used to refer to the reforms. The goals of the study were to make clear how school reform occurred in Chicago—showing the actual changes in the student population and teacher workforce at the schools—and to learn whether these efforts had a positive effect on student learning overall.

Overview of Reform Models in Chicago

Since 1997, CPS has initiated five distinct reforms that aim to dramatically improve low-performing schools in a short time. In chronological order, these models of reform are:

- Reconstitution model (seven high schools)
- School Closure and Restart model (six elementary schools and two high schools)

- School Turnaround Specialist Program (STSP) model (four elementary schools)
- Academy for Urban School Leadership (AUSL) model (10 elementary schools and two high schools)
- CPS Office of School Improvement (OSI) model (two elementary schools and three high schools).[2]

All initiatives relied on changing the school leadership. The main lever of change under the STSP model was through the school principal; administered by the University of Virginia's Partnership for Leaders in Education, the STSP focuses on the leadership aspect of low-performing schools by training principals to be "turnaround specialists." This reform is similar to the federal *transformational model*, in which one of the requirements is the replacement of the school principal. While the UVA model does not require replacement of the school principal, all but one of the schools that underwent this reform in Chicago did so.

Three other CPS models relied on changing both the leadership and the school staff. These are the Reconstitution, AUSL, and OSI models. Schools start the new academic year with dramatic changes to staffing, but the same students remain assigned to the schools. These reforms are similar to the federal *turnaround model*, which includes, among other actions, replacing the principal and at least 50 percent of the school's staff, adopting a new governance structure, and implementing a new or revised instructional program. The Reconstitution, AUSL, and OSI models implemented in CPS all shared some of these elements.

The last model, School Closure and Restart, was the most drastic intervention for several reasons: schools were closed for a year and students were moved into other schools. Subsequently, new schools opened in the same buildings as charter, contract, or performance schools. Student enrollment in the new schools required an application and lottery system. In most cases, the new schools opened with a few grades at a time and added a grade every year until the full grade structure was in place. This reform effort is similar to the federal *restart model*, in which schools are closed and reopened under the management of a charter school operator, a charter management organization, or an educational management organization.

The fourth federal model is *school closure*. In this model, schools are closed and students are sent to other schools in the district. While some schools in the district were closed permanently and students were displaced to other schools, these schools are not studied in this report since the schools remain permanently closed. A prior CCSR study examined the outcomes of students who attended schools that were closed; it showed that displaced students in Chicago tended to transfer from one low-performing school to another.[3] Overall, closings had no effect on student learning for displaced students.

Main Findings

Elementary schools that went through reform made significant improvements in test scores compared with similar schools that did not; however, large improvements in achievement did not occur immediately. In the first year of reform, improvements in reading and math test scores were only marginally higher than those at comparison schools, but in both reading and math almost all schools that underwent reform showed progress during the four years after reform. The gap in test scores between reformed elementary schools and the system average decreased by nearly half in reading and by almost two-thirds in math four years after the intervention took place. These trends are net of changes in student population that the schools might have experienced. That is to say, the analysis adjusts for the fact that some schools did not serve the same students before and after the intervention.

High schools that underwent reform did not show significant improvements in absences or ninth grade on-track to graduate rates over matched comparison schools, but recent high school efforts look more promising than earlier ones.[4] On average, there were no significant improvements in ninth grade on-track rates and absence rates among the schools that went through intervention. While on-track rates have improved system-wide over the last several years, on-track rates did not improve more in schools that underwent reform compared to similar schools that did not undergo reform. There was a drop in absence rates in the first year after reform compared to matched schools, but the improvement was not sustained over time.

Many of the high schools in this study went through the Reconstitution model in the late 1990's, and there were no improvements in attendance or on-track rates that accompanied this reform model. CPS administration recognized the problems with earlier attempts at reconstitution, and many of the reconstituted schools were again targeted for reform in subsequent years.

More recent attempts at high school reform have paid close attention to school organization. As yet, there are only seven high schools that experienced reform models other than Reconstitution, and several of them have only been in existence for one or two years. We are hesitant to make sweeping conclusions based on such a small number of schools with limited data. Among those schools with at least one year of data, however, six out of seven showed some improvement in on-track rates above the comparison schools. Most of the high schools reformed in recent years also showed a decline in absence rates in their first year, although not in subsequent years.

Schools that underwent reform generally served the same students as before intervention, with the exception of one model of reform. With the exception of schools in the Closure and Restart model, schools reenrolled between 55 and 89 percent of students eligible to reenroll in the year after intervention—rates that were similar to their year-to-year reenrollment rates prior to intervention. These patterns held true in the second and third years following intervention as well. In fact, more students reenrolled in subsequent years than in the first year of reform. All but one school served predominantly African American students with high levels of poverty. The composition of students in intervention schools—in terms of race/ethnicity, socioeconomic status, and special education status—was similar before and after intervention. These data contradict claims made by critics who argue that turnaround schools systematically push out low-performing and more disadvantaged students when schools undergo the transformation and turnaround models. Concerns about who the schools serve are valid, however, for the Closure and Restart model.

Schools under the Closure and Restart model experienced substantial changes to their student body composition, serving more economically advantaged students, students of higher prior achievement, and fewer special education students. After intervention, schools under the Closure and Restart model also served fewer students from the neighborhood around the school.

The vast majority of teachers in schools under Closure and Restart, AUSL, and OSI models were not rehired after reform. These schools rehired less than 10 percent of the teachers from the year before intervention. This is consistent with the theory of change behind the federal restart and turnaround models, which require that at least half of the staff change. In contrast, most schools in the Reconstitution model rehired about half of their teachers. Schools that were reconstituted had only a few months for planning and hiring new staff, and this may account for the larger percentage of teachers who were rehired. **The teacher workforce after intervention across all models was more likely to be white, younger, and less experienced, and was more likely to have provisional certification than the teachers who worked at those schools before the intervention.**

How Should We View These Results?

The results of this study suggest that turning around chronically low-performing schools is a process rather than an event. It does not occur immediately when staff or leadership or governance structures are replaced, but it can occur over time. We cannot determine whether the improvements came about because of the changes in staff, concerted planning, or extra resources in these schools or whether it was the combination of all of these factors.

Other studies have suggested that successful efforts to turn around low-performing schools usually do so by building the organizational strength of the school over time, using staff changes as just one of many mechanisms to improve school climate and instruction. A list of recommendations compiled in the IES Practice Guide on School Turnaround[5], based on case studies of schools that showed substantial improvement, starts with establishing strong leadership focused on improving school climate and instruction, strengthening partnerships across school communities, monitoring instruction, addressing discipline, and building distributed leadership among teachers in the school. The second recommendation is to maintain a consistent focus on improving instruction by having staff collaborate around data to analyze school policies and learning conditions. The third recommendation is to pursue quick wins that target critical but immediately addressable problems, including student discipline and safety, conflict in the school community, and school beautification. The final recommendation is to build a committed staff that is dedicated to school improvement through collaboration. None of the schools highlighted in the IES practice guide as successful examples of school improvement changed its entire staff, but all of them replaced teachers who did not share a commitment to change.

This is consistent with research at CCSR examining 100 elementary schools that made significant progress over a seven-year period—and 100 more that did not. The research found that schools strong on at least three of five essential elements—effective leaders, collaborative teachers, strong family and community ties, ambitious instruction, and safe and orderly learning climate—were 10 times more likely to improve and 30 times less likely to stagnate than those that were strong on just one or two.[6] Perhaps it is not surprising, then, that the recent reform models, OSI and AUSL—both of which have explicit blueprints for reform focused on building the organizational strength of schools—achieved consistent improvement in all of the elementary schools they managed.

Continued study will be needed to know whether these gains are sustained beyond the first four years, particularly if attention and resources from the district start to fade. These schools started out with extremely low levels of student performance and presented significant barriers to reform. A prior study at CCSR showed that over the past 20 years, CPS schools that started out with the lowest performance were the least likely to show improvement over time.[7] From this perspective, this study provides promising evidence about efforts to improve chronically low-performing schools—showing improvements in schools that historically have been most impervious to reform. At the same time, it tempers claims that these reforms bring quick, dramatic change—improvements were gradual and grew over time.

Introduction

Despite a recent federal focus on school turnaround efforts, there is little rigorous research on the impact of such reforms to date, and a need for greater understanding of how schools, teachers, and students are affected when a school is turned around.

The topic of "turning around" chronically low-performing schools has become prominent in national education discourse. The U.S. Department of Education (2009), independent researchers, school districts, and practitioners are calling for drastic improvement in the academic performance of these schools.[8]

National leaders have recently amplified the attention given to the school turnaround effort by defining and promoting four models that involve "dramatic change, including fundamental, comprehensive changes in leadership, staffing, and governance."[9] Currently, several competitive federal grants, including Race to the Top Fund grants and School Improvement Grants (SIGs), require recipients to implement one of these models. Moreover, the U.S. Department of Education recently substantially expanded funding for SIGs, with the stated goal of rapidly improving the nation's 5,000 lowest-performing schools.[10]

Despite the recent focus on turning schools around, there is little rigorous research on the impact of such reforms to date. Most studies of low-performing schools present a list of elements that are in place in schools that have implemented turnaround strategies.[11] These studies tend to draw on case studies of schools that have successfully "turned around," linking the success of such schools to the elements highlighted in the research. Although such studies are useful in describing what may be good practice for turning schools around, there is a need for greater understanding of the effects of turnaround reforms on schools, teachers, and students.

This lack of rigorous research is particularly problematic because these reforms are controversial, and efforts to enact them often raise considerable community opposition. There are strong advocates and opponents to these types of reform, but there is not enough information to validate the claims of either side.

To fill this gap in existing research, American Institutes for Research (AIR) and the University of Chicago Consortium on Chicago School Research (CCSR) have partnered to examine Chicago Public Schools (CPS) turnaround reform initiatives between 1997 and 2010.

CPS has been engaging in dramatic school improvement efforts for some time. Since 1997, the district has initiated at least five distinct reform initiatives that are similar to the sanctions listed in the 2002 reauthorization of the Elementary and Secondary Education Act (ESEA), commonly called the No Child Left Behind (NCLB) Act, for chronically low-performing schools. These sanctions include school-level changes in leadership, staff, and governance. The goal is to produce rapid, dramatic changes in chronically low-performing schools. U.S. Secretary of Education Arne Duncan led most of the efforts while he was the CEO of CPS, and these experiences were a precursor to the federal effort to turn around the lowest-performing schools in the nation. In fact, Chicago schools that underwent reform have been used as exemplars to show that such reforms can be successful.

There is little to no rigorous research on these schools, however, and this has raised a number of questions about the validity of these claims. Furthermore, there is confusion about which types of reform occurred in Chicago, and how various initiatives correspond to the models set forth by the federal government. This report examines Chicago schools that were chosen by the district for reform due to chronic low performance between the fall of 1997 and the fall of 2010.

In this report, we focus on district-mandated initiatives that were similar to the recommended school improvement models in the 2002 ESEA. Other reform efforts are not included in our study of student outcomes. For example, schools closed for low enrollment often underwent reforms that were similar to those in schools that were closed for low performance. We provide information on student demographics changes for these schools, but we do not examine changes in student outcomes. In addition, principals at other low-performing schools may have begun reform efforts in their own schools as a way to dramatically boost student achievement in a short time. For example 10 elementary schools in 2006 chose to get help from the nonprofit organization called Strategic Learning Initiatives in an effort to improve their schools. We do not study these school-led initiatives.

This report provides answers to four broad questions:

1. What types of reforms aimed at low-performing schools have occurred in Chicago, what are the levers of change in each effort, and how do these correspond with the models being promoted by the U.S. Department of Education?

With the idea of turning around low-performing schools gaining popularity in the country, it is important to understand different school intervention strategies in order to properly study their effects on schools and students. The U.S. Department of Education provided some clarity in November 2009 when it released a definition for a turnaround model in the Federal Register together with three other models aimed at the lowest-performing schools in the nation.

We provide a description of the strategies Chicago has used in the past, the models the federal government is promoting, and the similarities between the elements of each intervention in Chicago and the federal models.

2. Do the schools serve the same students after going through reform that they served prior to reform?

One question often asked about turnaround schools is whether they continue to serve the same students—or the same "type" of students. Parent and community groups often fear that these reforms push out neighborhood students. In addition, significant changes to student demographics make it hard to judge whether a school improved or simply reflected a higher performing incoming student body.

To address these issues, we compare students enrolled in September the year before intervention to the students enrolled in September in the first year of intervention. First, we determine whether the same students who were attending intervention schools before reform were there after reform. Next, we compare the characteristics of the student population before and after reform to identify differences in the types of students served.

3. To what extent was there a change in teaching staff with the reforms? How did the new teacher workforce compare to the previous one?

Some of the CPS initiatives, and some of the federal models, call for major personnel changes. A key feature of two of the models set out by the U.S. Department of Education is the restaffing of schools. The federal definition of school turnaround includes a mandate to "[s]creen all existing staff and rehire no more than 50 percent."[12] Large-scale restaffing seems to follow in the restart model as well as in schools that are closed and reopened under a charter or education management organization. Because staffing in low-performing schools has been and continues to be a focus of reform efforts, the third step in our study involves examining what types of staff changes occurred in Chicago's schools that underwent different models of reform.

Similar to the student population analysis, we compare the teacher workforce the year before intervention and the first year of intervention by asking how many teachers were rehired, and then comparing the characteristics of the teacher workforce before and after intervention.

4. To what extent did student outcomes change after intervention, relative to other similar schools in the district that did not go through intervention?
We analyze whether changes in student academic outcomes occurred after the interventions were in place in these low-performing schools using student assessment scores in elementary schools and two early warning indicators of high school graduation—absence rates and ninth-grade on-track to graduate rates.[13]

Although the models had different elements, the rationale behind all of them was to transform the culture and climate of failing schools and ultimately improve student outcomes. We did not attempt to study which models were more or less successful, but only whether these efforts as a group were related to improved student outcomes. Because there were a limited number of schools in any model, we were concerned that we would not have sufficient statistical power to make distinctions among them. The schools we studied were not a random sample of schools, nor were they randomly selected to undergo reform. Thus, the changes in student outcomes observed in these schools may not generalize to similar reform efforts in other schools or in other places.

We provide changes in student outcomes for individual schools, however, to check the degree to which improvements varied considerably across schools and types of reform. We consider them descriptive data of what happened at each school rather than providing causal information about a specific model of reform.

CHAPTER 1
Chicago's School Reform Efforts

The Chicago School Reform Amendatory Act (P.A. 89-15) was passed in 1995 in response to growing public dissatisfaction with student achievement. The legislation increased mayoral control and provided the school system with "enhanced powers over financial, managerial, and educational matters."[14] The authority granted to the district led to various reform initiatives aimed at poorly performing schools and increased the focus on school accountability and monitoring of schools, principals, and teachers in these poorly performing schools. Since the legislation was passed, school reform efforts in Chicago have become more focused on rapidly increasing student achievement in low-performing schools, in tandem with current national education policies and broader movements to turn schools around.[15]

This project focuses on the impact of several distinct and formal district-level initiatives put in place between 1997 and 2010 to dramatically improve schools' performance in a short amount of time:

- Reconstitution
- School Closure and Restart
- Leadership training in School Turnaround Specialist Program (STSP)
- Governance by Academy for Urban School Leadership (AUSL)
- Governance by Office of School Improvement (OSI)

Table 1 identifies the characteristics of each reform effort in Chicago. As of 2010, 36 CPS schools serving students in grades K-12 have undergone at least one of these initiatives. These schools were identified as chronically low performing during the period from 1997 through 2010 and meet the requirements of school interventions reserved for the lowest-performing schools in the nation as defined by the U.S. Department of Education.[16] Some schools experienced more than one intervention model at different points in time between 1997 and 2010. Detailed descriptions of the schools are in **Appendix A**.

TABLE 1

Five school improvement reform initiatives in CPS, 1997-2010

	Staff Replacement	Leadership Replacement	Governance Replacement	Change in Attendance Rules	Sample and Timing*
Reconstitution	X	X			7 HS (1997)
School Closure and Restart	X	X	X	X	6 ES; 2 HS (2002-2009)
School Turnaround Specialist Program		X			4 ES (2006)
Academy for Urban School Leadership	X	X	X		10 ES; 2 HS (2006-2010)
Office of School Improvement	X	X			2 ES; 3 HS (2008-2010)

* **ES** = Elementary School (schools serving any of the grades K through 8 but not serving students in the high school grades)—one of the schools under the STSP model was a middle school serving grades 7 and 8.
HS = High School (schools serving at least some of the grades 9-12).

Reconstitution

Reconstitution is an intervention model that began in the summer of 1997. This intervention was implemented over a brief period of time—changes occurred during the summer of 1997. All faculty and staff members from seven low-performing high schools were removed from their positions and were required to reapply for their jobs; those who were not rehired were replaced over the summer. Four of the schools' principals were replaced, and three principals were rehired for their previous positions.[17] This model followed the district's newly adopted Design for High Schools (which applied to all CPS high schools), which focused on academic press and personalization as two main drivers of change. Specific strategies in these areas included revised academic standards and frameworks and the introduction of career academies and student advisories. Reconstituted schools differed from other high schools in that they employed a third lever of change: replacement of staff members. In addition, these seven schools, and all other schools on academic probation, were assigned a probation manager (a veteran administrator) by the district and were able to select external partners (universities or consultants) with whom to work.[18] The goal of reconstitution was to increase student performance on state tests, though it is unclear whether any specific targets or timelines were set by individual schools or the district.[19] Reconstitution in this form has not been used since. Some of the seven reconstituted schools were identified for other types of reform in later years.

School Closure and Restart

Since 2002, six elementary schools and two high schools have been closed for low academic performance.[20] Tenured teachers were reassigned, untenured teachers and other staff members were laid off, and the schools remained closed for at least one academic year before reopening as new schools. More than 95 percent of the displaced students remained in CPS public schools, most often attending other neighborhood schools.[21] The closed schools then reopened as charter, contract, or performance schools, often as multiple-campus buildings, and new staff members were hired.[22] All the schools reopened with new names and were open to students throughout the city by a lottery process.

Many of the restart schools served different grade levels from those served by the schools they replaced. Two of these schools, one elementary and one high school, were designated professional development schools for the teacher training program run by the Academy of Urban School Leadership (AUSL). Although not included in this study, in 2012, the district identified two elementary schools to be closed and two high schools that will start a phase out process. One of the high schools will house two other schools in the next years. (For details about changes in each of the schools, **see Appendix A**.)

The majority of new schools were opened under Chicago's Renaissance 2010 (Ren10) initiative, through which they received "more freedom than traditional public schools in return for high levels of accountability."[23] For their charters to be renewed after five years, the new schools were required to meet targets for composite and growth scores on state tests, attendance, and graduation rates. Renaissance schools also received financial support for one to three years of as much as $500,000.

School Turnaround Specialist Program (STSP)

In 2006, four low-performing elementary schools were placed in the School Turnaround Specialist Program (STSP), administered by the University of Virginia's Partnership for Leaders in Education. The STSP focused on the leadership aspect of low-performing schools by training principals to be "turnaround specialists." Three of the schools received new principals, and the principal of one school remained in place. All four principals participated in an off-site training program that focused on best practices in education and business, including analyzing data, decision making, setting targets, and creating action plans.[24] Each principal had four goals: meet AYP requirements, reduce the reading failure rate by at least 10 percent, reduce the math failure rate by at least 10 percent, and receive a "meets" or "exceeds" on his or her annual evaluation from the area instructional officer.[25] In addition, each school set specific goals in areas such as academic achievement, attendance, parent involvement, professional development, and student discipline referrals. To help with this process, principals received a number of supports and incentives, including an additional $100 in funding per student in the 2006-07 and 2007-08 school years; consulting visits from an experienced administrator; a signing bonus; and a special contract that included graduated bonuses for meeting two, three, or four of the previously described targets.[26]

Academy for Urban School Leadership (AUSL)

Between the fall of 2006 and the fall of 2010, 10 low-performing elementary schools and two low-performing high schools were placed under AUSL, a local school management organization charged with the training of teachers to affect whole-school transformation. AUSL has a residency program, which combines a yearlong mentored teaching program at an AUSL-administered school in Chicago and evening graduate-level courses. The schools placed under AUSL terminated existing staff and replaced them with new staff members, most of whom were trained in the AUSL residency program. The schools placed under AUSL also hired new principals who were committed to the model. AUSL's improvement model, known as PASSAGE, has the following components: positive school culture, action against adversity, setting goals and getting it done, shared responsibility for achievement, guaranteed and viable curriculum, and engaging and personalized instruction. Tailored goals were created for each school, with a focus on increasing attendance and student achievement on state tests and decreasing incidents of student misconduct.[27] Schools undergoing the AUSL model were supported with additional funding from a variety of sources (e.g., CPS, grants such as the Teacher Quality Partnership grant, and major donors such as the Bill and Melinda Gates Foundation), enabling the district and schools to hire additional staff members, organize programs such as youth guidance, and undergo building renovations.[28] In the fall of 2012, six more elementary schools were placed under this model, but they are not included in this study.

Office of School Improvement (OSI)

Between 2008 and 2010, the district identified two low-performing elementary schools and three low-performing high schools to be turned around with the OSI model. Teachers in these schools were terminated at the conclusion of the school year, and new faculties were hired during the summer. Although not included in this study, in the fall of 2012, four more schools were placed under OSI: two elementary schools and two high schools. In four of the first cohort of OSI schools, the principal was replaced; in one school, the previous year's principal remained. Their model focuses on six distinctive areas of school organization and is implemented in a phased approach. The OSI model focuses first on stabilizing the school and developing a positive climate and culture in the building. At the end of the first year of turnaround, the focus turns to teaching and learning. The six elements of their model are school stabilization, school culture and climate, human capital, family and community involvement, community resource development, and teaching and learning. The schools under this model received additional financial support over five years, with levels of additional financial support intermittently dropping.[29] The overall goal of the model is to achieve significant gains on state assessments in Year 2,[30] as well as increases in attendance rate, graduation rate, and parent satisfaction, with a decrease in student misconduct.

Although schools were identified as chronically low performing and selected to undergo a particular reform, they were not the only low-performing schools in the district. Criteria has never been clearly stated for why these schools were selected and other schools were not selected. In more recent years, CPS reports that the district CEO may consider closing schools or enacting "other turnaround measures" if a school fails to earn at least 33.3 percent of available performance points under the district Performance Policy for two consecutive years.[31] If a school meets an exclusion factor, however, it will be removed from consideration. Exclusion factors include:

- For an elementary school, the contract principal has been in place for two years or fewer.
- The school is subject to an agreement with the Chicago Teachers Union that prohibits closure on the basis of academic reasons.
- The school has served as a receiving school for reassigned students as a result of a school closure or consolidation in the last two years.

- There are no schools within 1.5 miles of students' homes that have performed better under the CPS Performance Policy with safe passage unimpeded by unsafe natural barriers, or it is impractical to transport transitioning students to higher performing schools with available space that can meet the students' educational needs.

In addition, the CEO may consider feasibility factors that include limitations of space, facility conditions, and the ability to provide appropriate services in schools that would receive students from a closed school.

Since 2000, Chicago has closed many schools in the district for reasons other than low academic performance. The district policy establishes that schools can be closed for three different reasons: nonacademic reasons (e.g., low enrollment, building issues), academic reasons (e.g., low performance), and changes in the educational focus of a school. Many of the schools closed for low utilization or for change in educational focus have reopened later, but they are not the object of our study since the district did not identify them as low performing. In many cases, however, schools closed for low utilization or changes in educational focus were performing at levels that were similar to schools that were closed for low performance.[32] (For a list of these schools and an analysis of how student population changed in these schools, **see the box *What Happened to Schools that Closed for Low Utilization?*, p. 26.**) Many of the schools closed for changes in educational focus have been reopened as high schools under the Chicago High School Redesign Initiative (CHSRI).[33] CCSR has studied this reform in the past and found positive impacts in the attendance and graduation rates for students in these schools.[34]

School Intervention Models: Chicago Reforms and Federal Models

In November 2009, the U.S. Department of Education released in the Federal Register[A] the description of four school intervention models aimed at the persistently lowest-performing schools in the nation. The four models are the *turnaround model* (replacement of the principal and at least 50 percent of the school's staff); the *restart model* (schools close and reopen under the management of a charter school operator, a charter management organization, or an educational management organization); the *school closure model* (students enroll in other, high-achieving schools in the district); and the *transformational model* (replacement of the principal). Each is described in detail below.

Turnaround Model

In this model, the changes required to occur as outlined by the U.S. Department of Education are:

- Replace principal and grant the principal operational flexibility to run the school
- Screen existing staff, rehire no more than 50 percent of existing staff, and select new staff
- Implement strategies to recruit and retain staff to meet student needs and provide adequate professional development designed to build capacity and support staff
- Adopt new governance structure
- Select and implement an instructional model backed by research
- Support the use of student data to inform and differentiate instruction
- Provide increased learning time
- Provide social-emotional and community-oriented services and supports

Schools implementing the turnaround model may also implement any of the required or permissible strategies under the transformational model.

Restart Model

In this model, schools are closed and then reopened under a charter school operator, a charter management organization, or an education management organization. A requirement is that the reopened school must enroll, if possible given the grade structure, former students who want to attend the school.

School Closure Model

In this model, a school is closed and the displaced students are enrolled in higher-achieving schools within reasonable proximity to the closed school. Charter schools and new schools, even if achievement data are not yet available, might enroll these students.

Transformational Model

In this model, the changes proposed are outlined under four major categories:

1. **Develop and increase teacher and school leader effectiveness**

   - Replace principal
   - Implement new evaluation system for teachers and principals by taking into account, among other factors, data on student growth
   - Identify and reward staff who are increasing student outcomes; support and if necessary remove those who are not
   - Provide professional development designed to build capacity and support staff
   - Implement strategies to recruit and retain staff

2. **Adopt comprehensive instructional reform strategies**

   - Select and implement an instructional model backed by research
   - Promote the use of student data to inform and support differentiate instruction

3. **Increase learning time and create community-oriented schools**

   - Provide increased learning time
   - Provide social-emotional and community-oriented services and supports

4. **Provide operational flexibility and sustained support**

   - Give school operational flexibility
   - Give school technical assistance by the district or by a designated external partner

There is also a list of other permissible activities that schools under this model may implement.

SCHOOL INTERVENTION MODELS... *CONTINUED*

Even though the school intervention models used in Chicago occurred prior to the release of the federal definitions and do not fit the federal definitions perfectly, their main elements make them very similar. It was not until the fall of 2006 that Chicago used the term "turnaround schools" when Sherman Elementary began a turnaround process through AUSL that involved a new principal, re-staffing, and a focus on instructional improvement. The AUSL model, the OSI model, and the earlier Reconstitution efforts, contain the elements of the federal *turnaround model*.

Also, in 2006, four other CPS schools began an intervention through the STSP model that involved specialized training for principals and a focus on project management and data tracking, but no re-staffing. This model contains the elements of the federal *transformational model*.

Finally, the closing and reopening of schools, often accompanied by new personnel, leadership, and governance, is analogous to the federal *restart model*.

Research Methods in This Study

Analyses of Changes to Student Population and Teacher Workforce

In order to examine changes in the student body composition in schools targeted for reform, we compared the students who attended schools in September of the year before the intervention took place with those in September of the first year of the intervention. First, we examined whether students who were enrolled in the year before the intervention, and could have returned after intervention, did return. Only students who still could have enrolled in a grade served by their school were included for this analysis. Eighth graders entering ninth grade would be excluded in the schools serving only up to eighth graders. Second, we examined whether the composition of students served at the school changed after reform, comparing students enrolled after the reform to students enrolled in the same grade prior to reform.

Data on student body composition come from individual student administrative records that CCSR receives from CPS, including student race, age, gender, prior academic achievement, and special education status **(see Appendix B** for a description of the data and data sources). We used students' home addresses to determine whether schools continue to serve students from the same neighborhoods, and we linked addresses to information from the census at the block-group level to create indicators of poverty and social status in students' census block group to determine whether the types of neighborhoods being served by the school changed after intervention.

It is important to note that because most schools that closed and reopened with different grade structures, our analyses included only similar grades. For example, School A may have been a 9-12 high school prior to closure but served only ninth grade upon reopening and added an additional grade each year. In that case, our analysis included a comparison of the new ninth grade students with the last group of ninth grade students to have gone through that school before intervention.

To examine changes in staffing, we compared the teacher workforce before and after intervention using personnel records from CPS **(see Appendix B** for details on data sources and variables). As with the analysis of students, we examined (1) whether teachers who were in the school prior to reform returned to teach at the school after reform, and (2) whether the composition of teachers at the school changed with reform. The personnel records contain information on degrees (bachelor's, master's, or doctorate); experience within CPS; demographic characteristics (e.g., age, race, gender); and certification information. CPS personnel records do not include information on charter schools or contract schools and, therefore, some schools are not included in this analysis. This was the case for some schools in the Closure and Restart model because some reopened as charter or contract schools.

RESEARCH METHODS... *CONTINUED*

Analyses on Student Outcomes

Reading and math achievement trends for elementary schools (grades three to eight) as well as absences (grades nine to 12) and on-track to graduate[B] (grade nine) trends for high schools were compared before and after the intervention took place. Two types of comparisons were used in a difference-in-difference approach:

1. **Comparing student performance in the schools before and after intervention; and**
2. **Comparing trends in the treated schools to a group of matched schools that did not experience the intervention.**

The matched group of schools had similar student performance as the reformed schools before intervention, and served similar types of students. Three different methods of choosing a matched comparison group were used to ensure that the conclusions would be the same regardless of which schools were used to make the comparisons. The analyses of student outcomes also took into account any changes in the background characteristics of students entering the schools over time, including changes in students' race, gender, socioeconomic indicators, prior achievement, grade level, age at grade, and disability status.

Math and reading scores come from standardized tests that CPS students take each year in grades three through eight. Until spring 2005, the Iowa Tests of Basic Skills (ITBS) were administered in CPS; after that the test was replaced by the Illinois Standard Achievement Test (ISAT). To make the scores comparable across tests, we converted them into standard deviations from the system mean in each year and for each grade. Thus, they can be interpreted as the degree to which students' scores were different from average in the system in that year. For example, a score of -0.50 means that students are performing one-half of a standard deviation below the system mean for students in their grade. Standardizing within each year provides an automatic adjustment for any system-wide trends that may have occurred across the years and should not be attributed to the intervention, differences in tests, or scoring of tests.

Test scores cannot be used to study high schools during the time frame of these reforms. Since 1997, tests were given at different grade levels (first to ninth and tenth graders, later to ninth and eleventh graders, and since 2001 only to eleventh graders) with no overlap in the grades tested from 1997 to 2010. Therefore, absences and on-track rates are examined here. Student absence rates were recorded by CPS in a slightly different manner in the years prior to 2007-08 compared to the years after 2007-08. In order to make measures comparable, we converted each student's absence rate into standard deviations from the system mean for each fall semester and grade. This makes the measure of absence rates consistent across all years included in this study; they can be interpreted as the degree to which students' absence rates for the fall semester were different from the average in the system for that year. The on-track to graduate variable was not standardized because it was measured in the same way for all years in the study, taking a value of zero for students off-track and a value of one for students on-track.

The analyses were conducted separately for elementary schools and high schools. The analyses did not differentiate between the different reform efforts; instead, they examined whether schools that underwent any of the interventions showed improvements in students' outcomes and compared them with matched schools that did not undergo intervention. The schools we studied were not a random sample of schools, nor were they randomly selected to undergo reform. Thus, the changes in student outcomes observed in these schools may not generalize to similar reform efforts in other schools or in other places. School-by-school data can be used to discern patterns across schools undergoing similar types of reform; these provide some insight into issues and successes that might help inform future efforts. These should be treated as descriptive information about what occurred at each school.

Details on the data, methods, and statistical models used for this study are provided in **Appendix B and Appendix C**.

CHAPTER 2

Students in the Schools after Intervention

Some of the school intervention models in Chicago were designed to improve student outcomes in schools while minimizing any disruption to students who were supposed to return to these schools after the summer. This was not the case with Closure and Restart, where the school admission policies changed with reform and the schools were not necessarily intended to serve the same students. Corresponding to these differences in policies, we find that most schools served the same students, with the exception of the schools under the Closure and Restart model. Schools that were closed and restarted served students who were from less disadvantaged neighborhoods, who were less likely to be old for grade, and who had higher prior achievement. Under all reform models, intervention schools tended to serve fewer students after than before reform.

> **More information about the student composition of the schools is available in Appendix C**
>
> The figures and tables in this chapter show changes in student characteristics rather than initial or final levels. Statistics on the student composition in each school before and after intervention are provided in Appendix C. **Table C.1 in Appendix C** shows student characteristics by school before and after intervention, as well as re-enrollment numbers. **Table C.2** shows the yearly re-enrollment rates during each of the three years that followed the intervention.

Changes in Student Populations

Most schools served fewer students per grade after intervention; many of the schools became smaller with reform. A comparison of student enrollment size in the grades that existed in the schools before and after intervention shows that 27 out of 36 schools served fewer students per grade during the first year of intervention, with five schools serving at least 25 percent fewer students (see Table 2.)[35]

Schools generally served the same students before and after intervention. With the exception of the schools in the Closure and Restart model, the majority of students who had been enrolled in the September before their school was targeted for intervention returned in September during the first year of intervention (**see Figure 1**). For Reconstitution, STSP, AUSL, and OSI models, the average student reenrollment across schools ranged from 55 to 89 percent. The reenrollment rates were similar to rates of year-to-year reenrollment in these schools prior to intervention, with the exception of one school in the OSI model, where the reenrollment rate was much lower in the first year of intervention. We also examined the reenrollment rates after the first year of intervention, which were similar to or higher than reenrollment rates in the first year. Thus, in most schools, the reforms did not lead fewer students to return to the school than in the prior year. In a number of schools, year-to-year reenrollment increased after reform.

The Closure and Restart schools, however, did exhibit lower reenrollment after reform: from 0 to 46.5 percent. Because they closed for a year or two, students were forced to enroll elsewhere for at least one year. In addition, the new lottery admission process that was used when these schools reopened may have deterred or prevented some students from reenrolling by adding the extra step of having to apply.

Schools under the Closure and Restart model experienced substantial changes to their student body composition, serving more students from more advantaged neighborhoods, fewer who were old for grade, and more with higher prior achievement. All other schools served a student population with very similar characteristics before and after intervention. We examined characteristics of students at the schools before and after intervention, including the average distance students traveled to school, student demographics and achievement, and socioeconomic characteristics

TABLE 2

Reenrollment after intervention and changes in size of student body

Intervention Model	School Name	School Enrollment in Comparable Grades				Percent Reenrolled from Those Eligible
		Grades Compared	Enrollment Before	Enrollment After	Percentage Change	
Reconstitution	DuSable HS	9-12	1,481	1,183	-20.1%	55.8%
	Robeson HS	9-12	1,371	1,179	-14.0%	62.3%
	Harper HS	9-12	1,631	1,476	-9.5%	59.5%
	Phillips HS	9-12	1,194	982	-17.8%	61.6%
	Englewood HS	9-12	1,366	1,061	-22.3%	58.4%
	King HS	9-12	827	679	-17.9%	60.9%
	Orr HS	9-12	1,306	1,060	-18.8%	56.8%
Closure and Restart	Dodge ES	K-8	312	359	15.1%	46.5%
	Williams ES	K-8	727	383	-47.3%	31.1%
	Howland ES	4-5	76	119	56.6%	15.5%
	Bunche ES	K-5	274	202	-26.3%	11.8%
	Englewood HS*	9	381	174	-54.3%	0.0%
	Morse ES	K-2	153	116	-24.2%	11.4%
	Frazier ES	K-5	299	272	-9.0%	8.9%
	Collins HS	9	326	214	-34.4%	0.0%
STSP	Ames MS	7-8	768	819	6.6%	88.6%
	Earle ES	K-8	548	480	-12.4%	64.1%
	Medill ES	K-7	219	173	-21.0%	72.1%
	Jackson ES	K-8	368	355	-3.5%	75.2%
AUSL	Sherman ES	K-8	559	587	5.0%	72.7%
	Harvard ES	K-8	494	490	-0.8%	68.1%
	Howe ES	K-8	559	491	-12.2%	68.9%
	Orr HS	9-12	1,379	1,190	-13.7%	65.2%
	Morton ES	K-8	255	238	-6.7%	57.1%
	Dulles ES	K-8	395	410	3.8%	76.6%
	Johnson ES	K-8	235	242	3.0%	63.1%
	Bethune ES	K-8	318	341	7.2%	70.9%
	Curtis ES	K-8	424	417	-2.7%	70.0%
	Deneen ES	K-8	445	439	-2.4%	69.4%
	Bradwell ES	K-8	609	663	8.9%	65.1%
	Phillips HS	9-12	744	685	-8.0%	69.1%
OSI	Copernicus ES	K-8	353	313	-11.3%	63.5%
	Fulton ES	K-8	577	591	2.4%	64.6%
	Harper HS	9-12	1,274	946	-25.7%	55.3%
	Fenger HS	9-12	1,212	1,187	-2.1%	73.8%
	Marshall HS	9-12	996	775	-22.2%	65.7%

Note: *Two high schools opened in this building in two subsequent years. Enrollment After numbers include only one school, the one that opened first.

FIGURE 1

Percent of students who reenrolled after intervention (of those eligible)

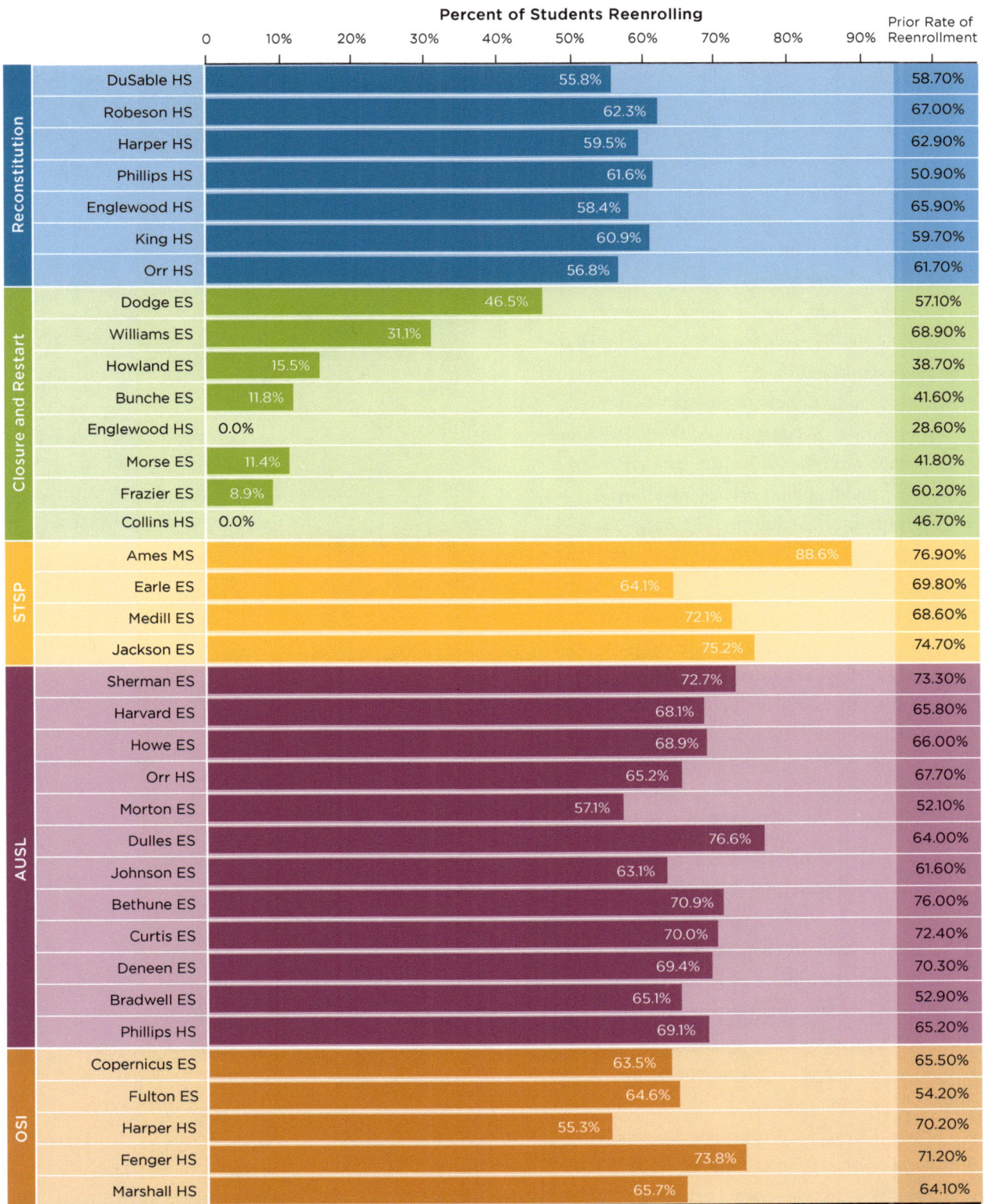

Note: The reenrollment rates in the final column are for a comparable time period prior to intervention. On Figures 1 through 7: The intervention models and the schools within each intervention model are placed in the order in which the reform efforts started in the schools and coordinated by color to indicate the different intervention models. The ordering of schools and intervention models is the same in all figures that depict changes in characteristics of students and teachers.

Chapter 2 | Students in the Schools after Intervention

of the neighborhoods where students lived. **Table 3** summarizes changes in the composition of students served by the schools.

- **Distance Traveled to School.** All Closure and Restart schools ceased to be neighborhood schools and instead started selecting students through a citywide lottery. These schools began serving students who lived on average between 0.25 miles and 1.36 miles farther from schools than the students in the year before intervention. This was not the case for the other reform models. Only two schools from other models saw an increase larger than 0.25 miles in the average distance traveled by their students to school.[36]

- **Neighborhood Concentration of Poverty and Social Status.** Reconstitution, AUSL, STSP, and OSI schools enrolled students who were from neighborhoods similar in concentration of poverty and social status to neighborhoods of students in the schools prior to intervention (**see Figure 2** and **see Appendix B** for an explanation of how these variables are calculated). Meanwhile, schools in the Closure and Restart model tended to serve somewhat more economically advantaged students; seven out of eight of the schools in the Closure and Restart model saw a decrease larger than 0.10 standard deviations in the average concentration of poverty where their students lived, and three out of eight saw an increase larger than 0.10 standard deviations in their students' neighborhood social status. For example, the change in neighborhood concentration of poverty for Bunche students changed from 1.16 standard deviations to 0.90 standard deviations; this corresponds to a change in the percentage of families above the poverty line from 49 percent to 61 percent, and a change in male unemployment from 57 to 51 percent.

- **Gender.** Changes in the proportion of male students ranged from declines of 5.3 percentage points to increases of 4.1 percentage points in Reconstitution, STSP, AUSL, and OSI schools. Six out of eight Closure and Restart schools saw changes larger than 5 percentage points.[37]

TABLE 3

Changes in student body characteristics after intervention

Intervention Model	School Name	Percent Male (% Point Changes)	Percent African American (% Point Changes)
Reconstitution	DuSable HS	3.4%	0.0%
	Robeson HS	1.2%	-0.4%
	Harper HS	1.1%	-0.3%
	Phillips HS	-4.3%	-0.3%
	Englewood HS	-3.0%	0.5%
	King HS	-2.3%	0.1%
	Orr HS	2.2%	-2.0%
Closure and Restart	Dodge ES	1.1%	-0.2%
	Williams ES	5.8%	0.0%
	Howland ES	7.6%	1.8%
	Bunche ES	-5.7%	0.7%
	Englewood HS*	40.4%	-0.1%
	Morse ES	-7.0%	-12.5%
	Frazier ES	1.3%	-1.5%
	Collins HS	-12.4%	-3.6%
STSP	Ames MS	-3.9%	0.2%
	Earle ES	0.5%	0.2%
	Medill ES	-0.1%	0.5%
	Jackson ES	0.6%	0.2%
AUSL	Sherman ES	0.1%	-0.8%
	Harvard ES	0.8%	-0.2%
	Howe ES	0.1%	0.0%
	Orr HS	1.1%	0.7%
	Morton ES	2.6%	-3.1%
	Dulles ES	1.9%	0.0%
	Johnson ES	-2.7%	0.9%
	Bethune ES	1.5%	0.6%
	Curtis ES	1.3%	1.2%
	Deneen ES	2.5%	-1.4%
	Bradwell ES	-1.6%	-0.7%
	Phillips HS	-0.3%	-1.3%
OSI	Copernicus ES	4.1%	0.5%
	Fulton ES	1.3%	-0.8%
	Harper HS	-5.3%	0.2%
	Fenger HS	-1.5%	0.0%
	Marshall HS	0.4%	-0.4%

Note: * Two high schools opened in this building in subsequent years. Changes in student body characteristics are based on the enrollment in the school that opened first in that building. One high school, formerly in the Englewood building turned into an all-male school.

Percent Latino (% Point Changes)	Percent Old for Grade (% Point Changes)	Percent Special Education (% Point Changes)	Average Neighborhood Concentration of Poverty (in Standard Deviations)	Average Neighborhood Social Status (in Standard Deviations)	Average Distance Traveled to School (miles)	Average Incoming Reading Performance (in Standard Deviations)
0.1%	-9.0%	4.2%	0.00	0.03	NA	0.00
0.2%	0.8%	3.6%	0.02	0.01	NA	0.02
0.2%	-4.0%	1.2%	-0.01	-0.02	NA	-0.03
0.1%	0.6%	0.9%	-0.06	0.01	NA	0.01
-0.2%	-6.1%	1.3%	-0.02	0.06	NA	0.07
0.0%	-5.4%	0.8%	-0.04	0.06	NA	0.01
2.2%	4.4%	2.3%	0.01	-0.02	NA	0.05
0.0%	1.7%	-10.1%	0.05	0.01	0.25	0.15
0.0%	7.1%	-1.7%	-0.15	0.07	1.04	-0.07
-1.8%	-32.4%	-4.6%	-0.71	-0.01	1.26	0.08
0.0%	-16.7%	-2.0%	-0.26	0.27	1.21	0.55
0.3%	-15.0%	-13.5%	-0.17	0.09	0.65	0.42
11.6%	-11.1%	-3.3%	-0.22	0.24	1.36	0.05
0.4%	-20.1%	-1.7%	-0.17	0.16	1.04	-0.05
3.6%	-25.7%	-7.2%	-0.22	0.01	0.35	0.23
0.1%	-0.3%	-1.3%	-0.01	0.01	0.10	0.05
0.0%	-0.5%	-2.3%	-0.01	0.03	0.09	-0.20
-0.5%	-2.8%	1.8%	-0.01	0.03	-0.19	-0.24
-0.2%	1.5%	-2.3%	0.00	0.00	-0.14	-0.09
0.5%	-1.5%	2.6%	0.01	0.03	0.00	-0.18
0.4%	-6.7%	-0.6%	0.05	0.04	-0.07	0.11
0.0%	-5.3%	-1.1%	-0.02	0.00	0.11	0.22
-0.4%	-6.8%	-1.0%	0.03	0.01	-0.04	0.01
2.7%	-4.0%	1.7%	-0.03	0.02	0.03	0.20
0.0%	-1.5%	-1.5%	-0.02	0.02	0.00	0.15
-0.9%	-1.8%	-2.5%	-0.04	-0.03	0.26	0.01
-0.6%	-1.6%	1.8%	0.03	0.02	-0.02	-0.05
-0.7%	0.9%	0.2%	-0.01	-0.01	0.02	-0.02
0.2%	-3.3%	1.3%	0.08	-0.08	0.24	0.05
0.4%	-4.1%	0.7%	-0.05	0.03	0.03	0.05
1.5%	-2.6%	-0.8%	-0.02	0.06	0.23	-0.04
-0.3%	-2.6%	-1.1%	0.04	-0.03	0.11	0.22
0.6%	-4.6%	1.0%	-0.01	0.02	0.05	0.05
-0.1%	-5.3%	-1.2%	0.00	0.02	0.04	0.05
0.1%	1.7%	-2.3%	0.05	0.00	-0.08	-0.01
0.4%	24.2%	-0.3%	-0.02	0.00	0.17	0.01

FIGURE 2

Changes in average school poverty level as measured by the concentration of poverty in students' neighborhoods

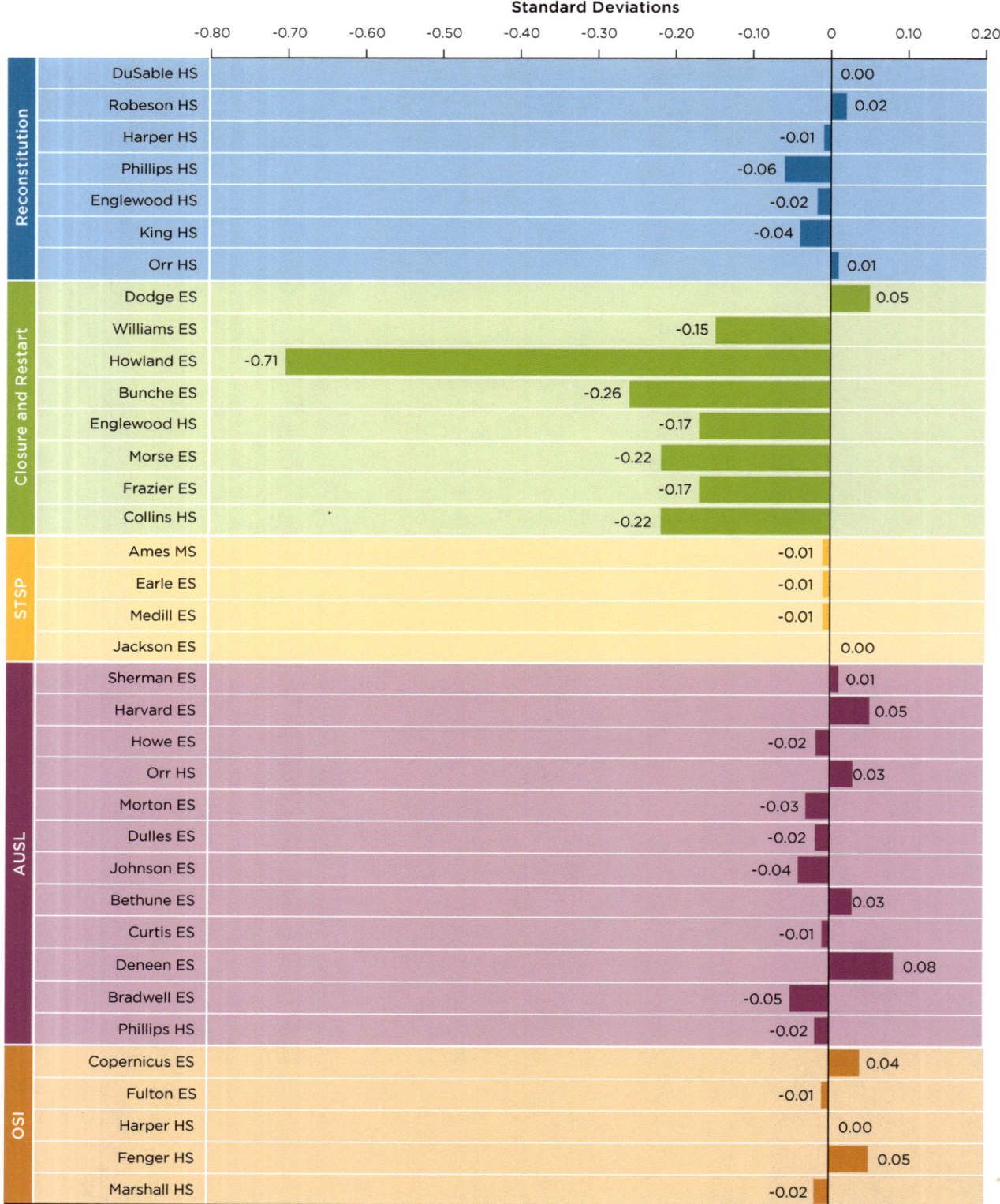

- **Race.** All but one school served mainly African American students. The racial composition of students was similar before and after intervention under these five intervention models, with the exception of Morse Elementary School, which saw the population of African American students decrease by 12.5 percentage points and an increase in their Latino students of 11.6 percentage points.
- **Old for Grade.** Each of the five categories of reform methods included schools in which the percentage of students who were old for grade decreased during the first year of intervention (**see Figure 3**). Schools undergoing the Closure and Restart model experienced the greatest decreases, with six of their eight schools decreasing their proportion of students who were old for grade by more than 10 percentage points. Schools undergoing the OSI, STSP, and AUSL models had smaller changes in the percentage of students who were old for grade, ranging from increases of 1.7 percentage points to decreases of 6.8 percentage points , with one exception. Marshall High School experienced an increase of 24.2 percentage points in terms of students old for grade. Students who are old for their grade often either were held back in grade or entered school later than expected.
- **Special Education.** The number of students receiving special education services remained similar after Year 1 of intervention in Reconstitution, STSP, AUSL, and OSI schools. Three out of eight Closure and Restart schools experienced decreases in the proportion of special education students greater than 5 percentage points after intervention.
- **Incoming Reading Performance.** Six out of the 36 schools saw increases of 0.2 standard deviations or more in their students' prior reading achievement (**see Figure 4**). These were three of the Closure and Restart schools, two of the AUSL schools, and one of the OSI schools. The largest change in prior achievement levels was at Bunche, where there was an increase of almost half of a standard deviation (from -0.46 to 0.09). This corresponds to a change that is equivalent to fourth graders coming in at the 41st percentile instead of the 23rd percentile. Two of the STSP schools saw decreases of 0.2 standard deviations or more in the students' incoming reading achievement from the reading achievement of the student population before the intervention.

FIGURE 3

Changes in the percentage of students old for grade

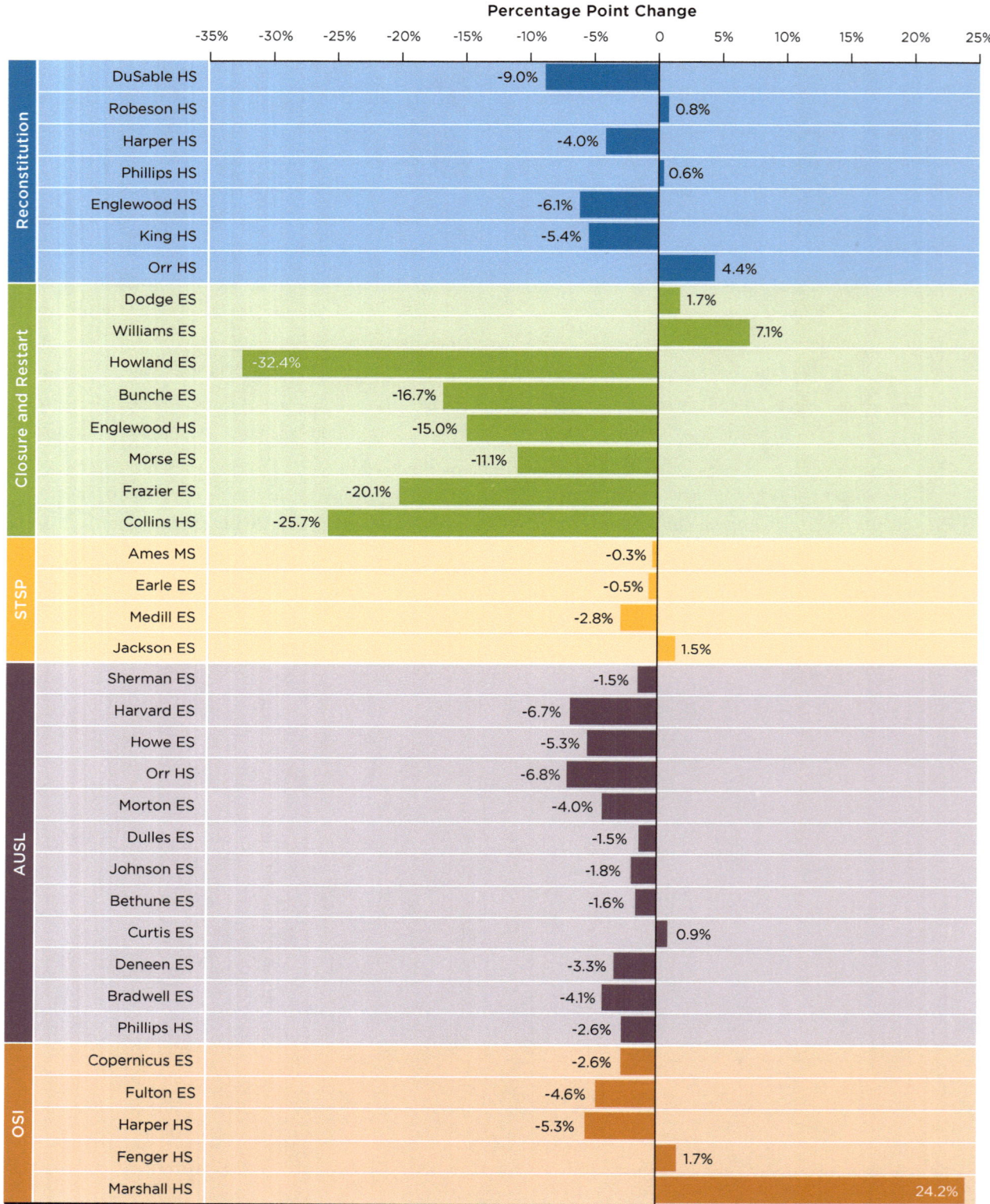

FIGURE 4

Changes in the incoming reading performance of students

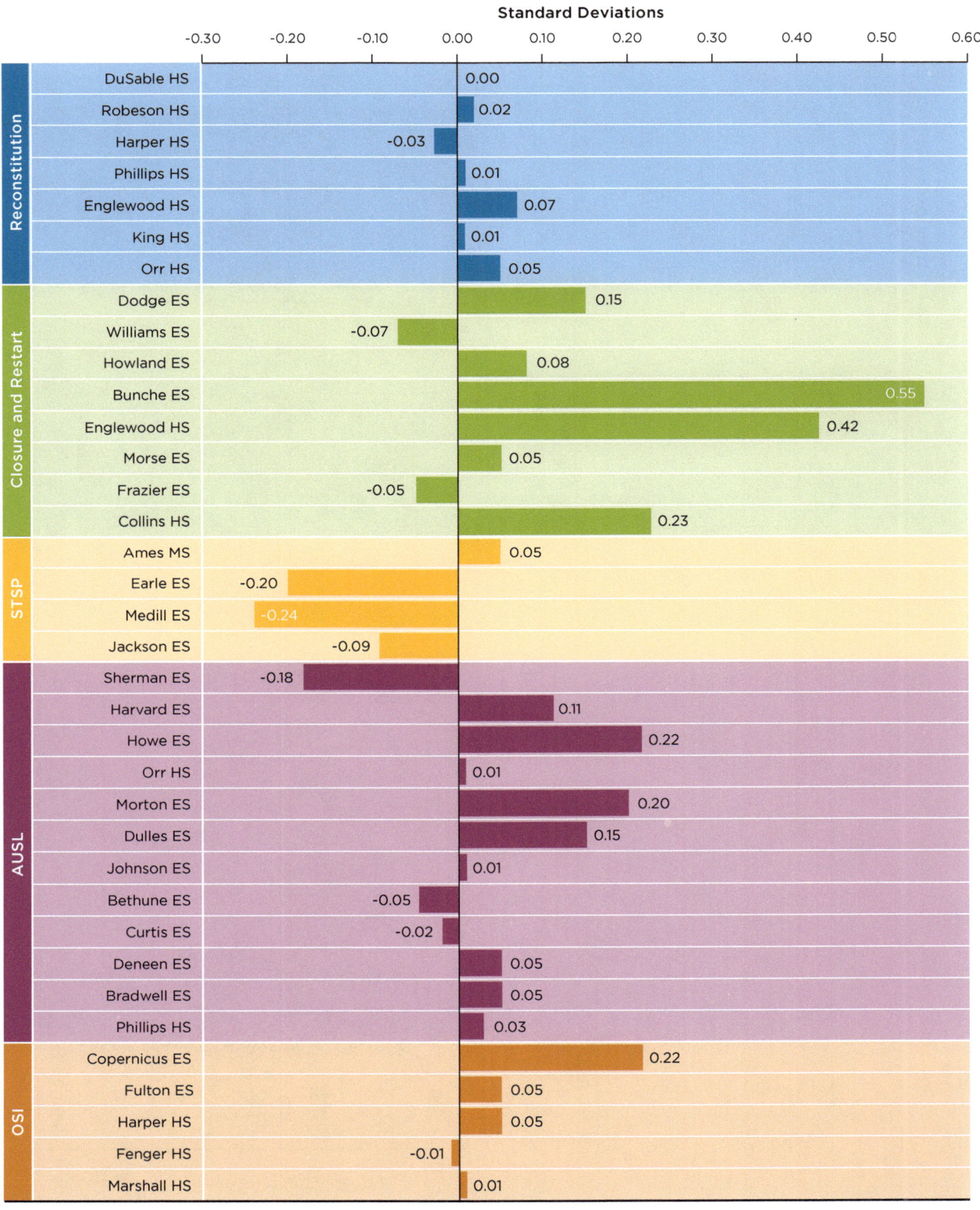

What Happened to the Schools Closed for Low Utilization?

At the same time that CPS closed schools for low performance, many other schools were closed for low utilization. CPS emphasized the financial necessity of closing schools where student enrollment was far below the intended capacity of that school. The attendance area boundaries for these schools were redrawn among schools nearby, with displaced students attending those schools as well as other schools in the district.

In many cases, the buildings of the closed schools housed other schools after a few years of the closing (see Tables A and B). In general, those schools were new schools that were usually designated as magnet or charter schools. Many were part of the Renaissance 2010 initiative, which aimed to open more than 100 high-quality schools by the year 2010. The reopening generally took place several years after the school closed, and the newly opened school did not always serve the same grades. As was the case with schools that closed for low performance and reopened, the new schools were not usually neighborhood schools and students needed to enter a lottery to attend.

Tables A and B show the schools that have been closed for underutilization since 2000. Where the newly reopened schools served similar grades, we can compare the students who were served in the building before and after reform (**Table A**). When schools closed for low utilization reopened, very few students returned. In most cases this was because the new school did not reopen until several years after closure. In the case of Davis, which did close and reopen in the same year, 77.3 percent of the students returned.

A comparison of the student population in these schools before closing and the first year the new school opened up shows similar patterns to the schools that closed for low performance and reopened as charter, contract, or performance schools, in that they tended to serve more advantaged students after reform. In the majority of the schools closed for underutilization, the newly opened schools served students from neighborhoods that were farther away from the school and less disadvantaged than the neighborhoods students came from before closure. The student body of the newly opened schools generally contained fewer students requiring special education services or old for grade, and students tended to have higher prior achievement levels.

Table B shows other schools closed for low utilization where either no school reopened or when the new school reopened it did not serve similar grades.

TABLE A

Changes in student population characteristics after new school

Closed School (Year Closed) Grades Served	Newly Opened School Name (Year Opened) Grades Served First Year (at full capacity) Type of School	Percent Students Reenrolling (of those eligible)	Percent Male (% Point Changes)
Douglas ES (2002-03) K-8	Pershing West MS (2005-06) 4-8(4-8) Magnet School	3.1%	1.5%
Woodson North ES (2002-03) K-8	UC Charter Woodson MS (2008-09) 6-8(6-8) Charter School	0.0%	-0.3%
Donoghue ES (2002-03) K-8	UC Charter Donoghue ES (2005-06) K-3(K-5) Charter School	0.0%	0.2%
Hartigan ES (2003-04) K-8	Bronzeville ES (2006-07) K-5(K-8) Charter School	6.3%	-2.8%
Suder ES (2003-04) K-8	Suder Montessori (2005-06) K(K-8) Magnet School	0.0%	-21.3%
Arai MS (2003-04) 6-8	UPLIFT HS (2005-06) 6-9(6-12) Neighborhood School	58.8%	-2.0%
Jefferson ES (2003-04) K-8	STEM ES (2011-12) K-3(K-8) Magnet School	0.0%	-0.9%
Raymond ES (2003-04) K-8	Perspectives HS (2008-09) 6-7,9(6-12) Charter School	0.0%	-5.8%
Davis ES (2007-08) K-3	Davis Magnet ES (2008-09) K-8(K-8) Magnet School	77.3%	-2.8%

Notes:
*Suder Montessori opened with one grade in 2005, kindergarten, for which achievement data is not available.

**Negative figures in concentration of poverty mean poverty decreased.

opened in buildings closed for low utilization

Changes in Student Characteristics							
Percent African American (% Point Changes)	Percent Latino (% Point Changes)	Percent Old for Grade (% Point Changes)	Percent Special Education (% Point Changes)	Average Neighborhood Concentration of Poverty** (in Standard Deviations)	Average Neighborhood Social Status (in Standard Deviations)	Average Distance Traveled to School (miles)	Average Incoming Reading Performance (in Standard Deviations)
-4.3%	3.0%	-24.1%	-11.4%	-0.35	0.26	0.90	0.05
0.6%	-0.1%	-20.2%	-12.8%	-0.42	0.44	2.14	0.11
-1.4%	0.7%	-10.4%	-12.5%	-0.65	0.43	2.62	0.09
-1.9%	1.3%	-9.1%	-5.2%	-0.57	0.54	2.06	0.03
-19.2%	13.6%	8.0%	8.1%	-0.98	0.33	2.02	n/a*
3.0%	-0.9%	-7.7%	-9.2%	0.00	0.08	0.13	-0.04
2.0%	0.7%	-21.4%	-10.8%	-0.52	0.48	1.43	0.16
-7.8%	5.8%	-36.1%	-14.1%	-0.92	0.78	3.44	-0.02
0.0%	0.0%	3.0%	1.7%	0.02	0.05	-0.10	0.07

WHAT HAPPENED TO THE SCHOOLS... CONTINUED

TABLE B

Other schools that closed for low utilization

Year	Closed School Name	Grades Served Before Closing	Newly Open School Name	First Year in Operation	Grades Served First Year (at full capacity)	Type of School
Closed at the end of 2000-01	Riis ES	K-8	Building Demolished			
Closed at the end of 2002-03	Colman ES	K-8	—			
Closed at the end of 2002-03	Arts of Living HS	6-12	—			
Closed at the end of 2002-03	Tesla HS	6-12	Woodlawn Community School (was already in same building)			
Phased Out at the end of 2003-04	Anderson Community Academy ES	K-8	—			
Closed at the end of 2003-04	Byrd ES	K-8	Housing a Catholic School			
Closed at the end of 2003-04	Doolittle West ES	K-4	ChiArts HS	Fall 2009	9(9-12)	Contract School
Closed at the end of 2003-04	Truth ES	K-3	Chicago International Charter HS Quest Campus	Fall 2012	6-8(6-12)	Charter School
Closed at the end of 2003-04	Spalding ES	4-8	Hope Institute Learning Academy	Fall 2008	K-3(K-12)	Special Education School
Closed at the end of 2003-04	Spalding HS	9-12	Hope Institute Learning Academy			
Closed at the end of 2006-07	Lemoyne ES	4-8	Inter-American Magnet ES (moved to building)	Fall 2006	K-8(K-8)	Magnet School
Phased Out Started at the end of 2007-08	Andersen ES	K-8	LaSalle II Language Academy (sharing building since 2007-08)	Fall 2007	K-8(K-8)	Magnet School
Closed at the end of 2007-08	De La Cruz MS	6-8	—			
Closed at the end of 2007-08	Irving Park MS	7-8	Disney II Magnet	Fall 2009	K-3(K-8)	Magnet School

TABLE B *CONTINUED*

Year	School Name	Grades Served Prior Change	New School Opened	First Year in Operation	Grades Served First Year (at full capacity)	Type of School
Closed at the end of 2007-08	Gladstone ES	K-8	Noble Street Charter-UIC	Fall 2008	9 (9-12)	Charter School
Closed at the end of 2007-08	Midway ES	K-8	Pasteur ES Branch (relieving overcrowding)			
Closed at the end of 2007-08	Johns Academy MS	4-8	Betty Shabazz International Charter School (Sizemore Academy was sharing building since fall 2005)	Fall 2005	K-3 (K-7)	Charter School
Closed at the end of 2008-09	Foundations ES	K-5	Noble Street Charter School-Chicago Bulls College Prep Campus	Fall 2009	9 (9-12)	Charter School
Closed at the end of 2008-09	Nia MS	6-8				
Closed at the end of 2008-09	Princeton ES	K-8	—			
Closed at the end of 2008-09	South Chicago ES	K-8	EPIC Academy	Fall 2009	9 (9-12)	Charter School
Closed at the end of 2010-11	McCorkle ES	K-8				
Closed at the end of 2010-11	Schneider ES	K-8	Alcott High School for the Humanities	Fall 2009	9 (9-12)	Performance School
Closed at the end of 2010-11	Avondale ES	K-5	Logandale School (consolidation of Avondale ES and Logandale MS–was sharing building)	Fall 2011	K-8(K-8)	Neighborhood School
Closed at end of 2010-11 (Phased Out 2008-09)	Carpenter ES	K-8	Ogden International HS	Fall 2009	9(9-12)	Performance School
Closed 2011-12	Reed ES	K-8	Noble Street-Johnson HS	Fall 2011	9(9-12)	Charter School

CHAPTER 3

Teachers in the Schools after Intervention

Most of the interventions studied in this report relied on major changes in the teacher workforce by either requiring teachers to re-apply for their jobs—as was the case for schools under the Reconstitution, AUSL, and OSI models—or closing and reopening schools where new teachers were hired. By examining teacher rehiring, we can better understand the degree to which schools used changes in personnel as a way to bring about changes in the schools. We find that the vast majority of teachers were not rehired under the Closure and Restart, AUSL, and OSI models, half or less than half of the teacher workforce was rehired in the Reconstitution schools. After intervention, the teacher workforce tended to be younger, less experienced, and have provisional certifications; they also were more likely to be white.

As with the student population analysis, we compare the teacher workforce the year before intervention and in the first year of intervention by first examining how many teachers were rehired, and then comparing the characteristics of the teacher workforce before and after intervention.

> **More information about the teacher composition of the schools is available in Appendix C**
>
> The figures and Table 4 in this chapter show changes in teacher characteristics rather than initial or final levels. Descriptive information about teacher characteristics before and after intervention are provided in Appendix C, Table C.3.
>
> Staff data are not available for all schools. Three Closure and Restart schools were converted to charter schools and we do not have access to staff data for charter schools. In addition, staff data for AUSL and OSI schools that were turned around after 2010 are not yet available.

Changes in Teacher Populations

Teacher rehiring practices varied considerably across models of intervention, with most schools retaining less than half of their teaching staff.
Of the five intervention models studied in this report, four—Reconstitution, OSI, AUSL, and Closure and Restart—included restaffing as a lever of change. Teachers were let go in those schools under the four intervention models and had the opportunity to reapply for their jobs in the schools under Reconstitution, OSI, and AUSL models. In the schools under reconstitution the rehiring process was left to the principals' discretion. AUSL schools largely hired teachers who underwent one year of training in the AUSL program. The OSI schools hired teachers from the open market using a six step process.[38]

- **Rehire/Retention Status.** The rehiring or retention of teachers varied considerably across interventions. The majority of teachers in schools undergoing the OSI and AUSL models were not rehired (**see Figure 5**) with nine out of the 12 schools for which data were available rehiring fewer than 10 percent of teachers. All schools in the Reconstitution model rehired more than 42 percent of their teachers.[39] Replacing faculty members was not used as a lever of change in the STSP model; between 20.7 and 56.2 percent of teachers, however, did not return the following year in the four schools. In the Closure and Restart model, four of the five schools for which data were available did not rehire any teachers, and the fifth school rehired 4.7 percent.

TABLE 4

Changes in teacher characteristics after intervention

Intervention Model	School Name	Percent Rehired/Retained	Change in Teacher Characteristics				
			Percent Male (% Point Changes)	Percent White (% Point Changes)	Percent African American (% Point Changes)	Percent Asian American (% Point Changes)	Percent Latino (% Point Changes)
Reconstitution	DuSable HS	66.3%	2.5%	4.1%	-3.4%	0.5%	-1.2%
	Robeson HS	47.4%	-4.3%	4.7%	-7.9%	3.2%	0.0%
	Harper HS	58.6%	-1.6%	-4.6%	6.9%	-2.3%	0.0%
	Phillips HS	42.9%	1.0%	-3.0%	-0.9%	2.2%	1.7%
	Englewood HS	46.3%	-10.3%	-11.6%	11.6%	0.0%	0.0%
	King HS	42.1%	-13.6%	1.2%	-1.2%	0.0%	0.0%
	Orr HS	49.5%	-5.0%	-7.3%	6.7%	0.3%	0.3%
Closure and Restart	Dodge ES	0.0%	-15.7%	9.8%	-9.8%	0.0%	0.0%
	Williams ES	4.7%	-9.6%	14.4%	-25.4%	10.0%	1.0%
	Howland ES	Not Available	NA	NA	NA	NA	NA
	Bunche ES	Not Available	NA	NA	NA	NA	NA
	Englewood HS*	0.0%	3.8%	56.3%	-45.5%	-2.7%	-5.4%
	Morse ES	Not Available	NA	NA	NA	NA	NA
	Frazier ES*	0.0%	-4.9%	38.7%	-30.7%	-8.0%	0.0%
	Collins HS*	0.0%	30.8%	27.6%	-25.3%	-2.3%	0.0%
STSP	Ames MS	70.2%	10.3%	-11.3%	3.7%	-1.9%	9.4%
	Earle ES	66.7%	8.9%	-2.4%	2.4%	0.0%	0.0%
	Medill ES	43.8%	7.1%	-20.5%	25.0%	8.0%	-12.5%
	Jackson ES	79.3%	-4.1%	-4.6%	4.6%	0.0%	0.0%
AUSL	Sherman ES	0.0%	0.0%	3.2%	-3.2%	-3.2%	3.2%
	Harvard ES	7.7%	8.6%	1.1%	-5.1%	0.0%	4.0%
	Howe ES	0.0%	-2.2%	28.1%	-30.7%	0.0%	2.6%
	Orr HS	23.5%	-7.6%	-16.2%	14.4%	-0.9%	2.4%
	Morton ES	9.1%	23.2%	34.8%	-41.4%	5.6%	1.0%
	Dulles ES	3.7%	1.9%	59.7%	-59.7%	0.0%	0.0%
	Johnson ES	0.0%	-13.2%	-2.6%	8.8%	0.0%	-6.3%
	Bethune ES	0.0%	-5.7%	22.3%	-24.7%	-1.4%	3.8%
	Curtis ES	Not Available	NA	NA	NA	NA	NA
	Deneen ES	Not Available	NA	NA	NA	NA	NA
	Bradwell ES	Not Available	NA	NA	NA	NA	NA
	Phillips HS	Not Available	NA	NA	NA	NA	NA
OSI	Copernicus ES	9.1%	-7.1%	6.1%	-8.1%	11.1%	-4.5%
	Fulton ES	5.4%	15.9%	23.6%	-23.4%	0.0%	2.5%
	Harper HS	17.5%	4.6%	4.8%	-12.6%	7.7%	0.0%
	Fenger HS	13.8%	-3.0%	17.2%	-16.5%	3.1%	-2.6%
	Marshall HS	Not Available	NA	NA	NA	NA	NA

Note: *Two schools opened up in these buildings, but data were available for only one of the schools. The second school was either a charter or a contract school.

Percent Advanced Degrees (% Point Changes)	Average Age	Average Years of CPS Service	Percent Provisional Certification (% Point Changes)
3.0%	-0.82	-0.58	-0.5%
-9.0%	-3.38	-4.36	7.4%
-1.5%	-1.04	-1.77	4.1%
-2.2%	-3.60	-3.38	-1.0%
4.4%	-2.87	-0.47	11.9%
-5.0%	-3.08	-1.53	5.1%
-0.1%	-3.14	-2.41	5.2%
24.8%	-4.90	-1.91	-9.1%
-11.2%	-12.67	-9.23	-4.7%
NA	NA	NA	NA
NA	NA	NA	NA
0.0%	-17.35	-10.64	30.6%
NA	NA	NA	NA
0.0%	0.81	-6.44	0.0%
0.0%	-15.68	-13.44	20.3%
-1.4%	0.21	0.56	5.0%
-20.8%	-1.12	-6.08	14.3%
16.1%	-0.01	-5.25	14.3%
-3.8%	0.34	-0.01	9.7%
19.4%	-7.26	-6.07	0.0%
0.0%	-10.91	-8.66	-3.7%
17.8%	-16.27	-8.68	-1.5%
1.2%	-0.04	-1.79	9.0%
28.3%	-9.59	-7.06	-2.5%
6.0%	-7.87	-11.88	12.5%
39.3%	-12.88	-7.63	-0.4%
12.8%	-6.00	-6.17	6.3%
NA	NA	NA	NA
NA	NA	NA	NA
NA	NA	NA	NA
NA	NA	NA	NA
12.1%	-3.24	0.73	14.1%
-0.4%	-9.61	-6.71	15.9%
-18.8%	-5.65	-7.99	14.4%
-13.7%	-4.26	-6.04	23.4%
NA	NA	NA	NA

After intervention, teaching staff tended to be younger, less experienced, and more likely to have provisional certification; schools tended to have more white teachers after intervention.

The demographics and qualifications of newly hired teachers across intervention models differed from those of the schools' previous faculties.

- **Age.** Teachers working in the schools after intervention were younger on average than teachers working in the schools prior to intervention. In all but three schools across the five models, the average age of teachers was lower than it was before intervention. In three of the models—Reconstitution and STSP being the exceptions—teachers were, on average, more than five years younger than faculty members from the previous year. Schools in the Closure and Restart model had the greatest change: the average teacher in these schools was about 40 years old—10 years younger than the average teacher prior to intervention.

- **Gender.** For the 28 schools with data, the percentage of male teachers hired at the intervention schools fell in 15 schools and rose in 12. The proportion of male teachers fell more than 10 percentage points in four schools and rose 10 percentage points or more in four other schools.

- **Race.** A greater proportion of teachers were white in 18 of the 28 schools after intervention (see **Figure 6**). In most of these 18 schools, the proportion of African American teachers declined. Ten schools in the Closure and Restart, AUSL, and OSI models saw increases in the percentage of white teachers of more than 10 percentage points, while the proportion of African American teachers in these schools decreased by 16.5 percentage points or more. As a result, faculties in these three models included nearly equal percentages of African American and white teachers after intervention, although they were mostly African American prior to intervention. Meanwhile, the number of white teachers decreased in four out of seven of the Reconstituted schools and all STSP schools. In these models, white teachers composed less than 30 percent of the faculties after intervention.

- **Years of CPS Service.** In the first year after intervention, teachers had fewer years of CPS service, on average, than their counterparts from the previous year (**see Figure 7**). In 16 of the 28 schools with available data, the decrease in the years of CPS service was greater than five years of experience.

- **Provisional Certification.** In 18 out of 28 schools, a greater proportion of teachers had provisional certification after intervention.[40] All the schools under the OSI model increased the percentage of teachers with provisional certifications by more than 14 percentage points.

- **Advanced Degrees.** Twelve of the 20 schools in the Reconstitution, STSP, Closure and Restart, and OSI models experienced declines in the number of teachers with advanced degrees. Seven out of eight schools in the AUSL model experienced increases in the percentage of teachers with advanced degrees; the increase ranged from 1.2 to 39.3 percentage points.

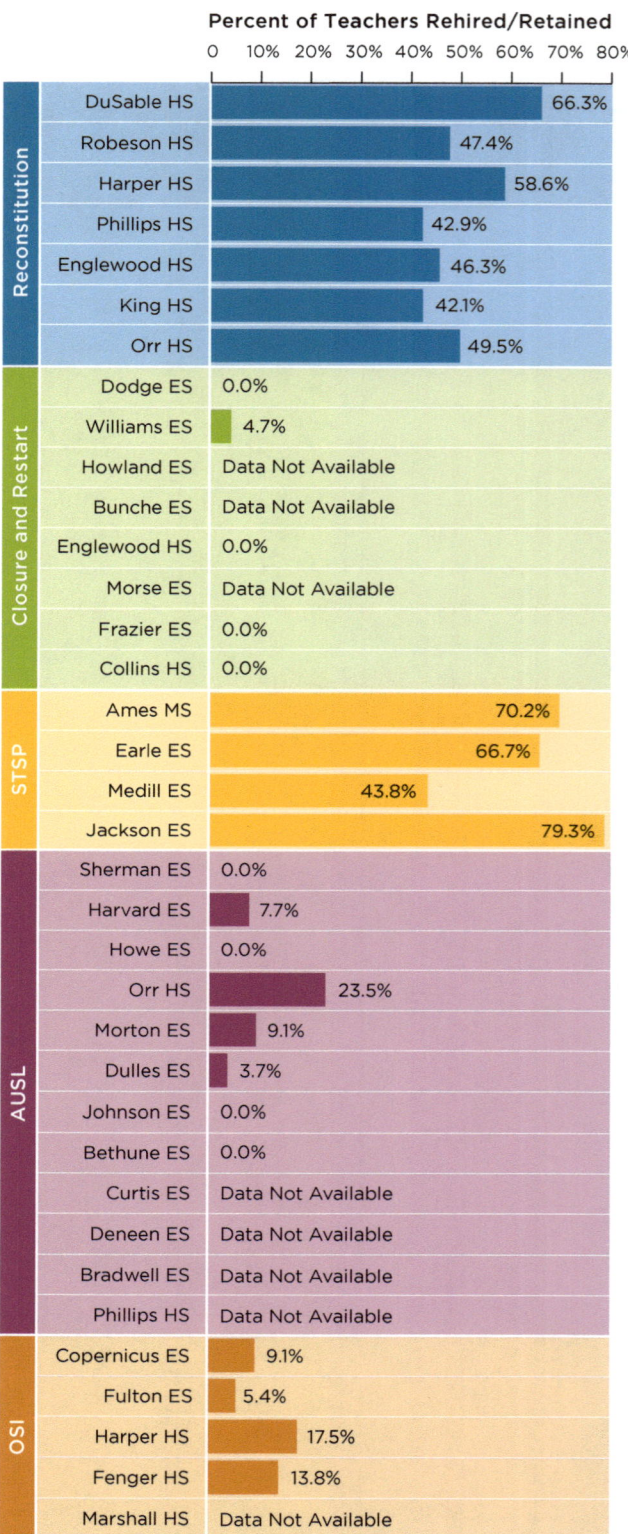

FIGURE 5

Percentage of teachers who were rehired/retained

FIGURE 6
Changes in the percentage of white teachers

FIGURE 7
Changes in the average years of CPS service

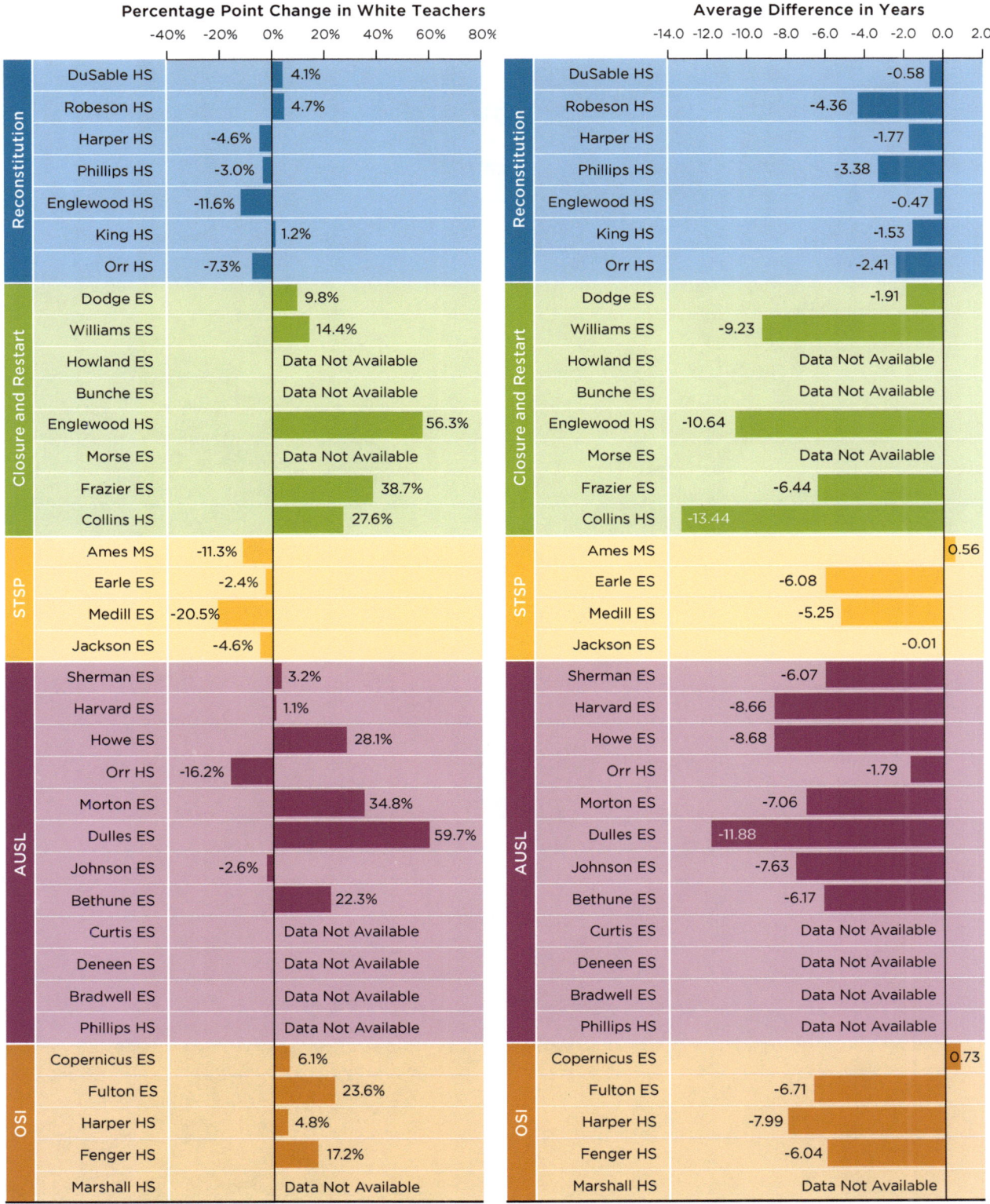

Chapter 3 | Teachers in the Schools after Intervention

CHAPTER 4

Student Outcomes in the Schools after Intervention

All of these interventions were implemented in the lowest-performing schools in the district with the goal of improving student outcomes. This chapter offers the results of the analyses on standardized achievement scores in reading and math for grades 3-8 and for absences for grades 9-12 and on-track to graduate indicator for grade 9. We find that elementary school test scores improved, both in reading and math. The changes took place gradually, but in time these schools reduced the gap with the system average by almost half in reading and almost two-thirds in math after four years. It is important to note that the analyses made adjustments for changes in the characteristics of students in the schools so that the estimated effects were net of student changes that took place in some of the schools. High schools, however, saw little improvement in absences and on-track to graduate rates. Some promising signs seem to be emerging around more recent initiatives when we delve into school-by-school changes.

How We Conducted the Analysis of Student Outcomes

This chapter presents a series of analyses comparing changes over time in student outcomes in schools selected for reform with schools that were similar to them before reform but not selected for intervention. The analyses made adjustments for changes in the background characteristics of students in the schools so that the effects were net of any changes in the students in the schools.

The comparison group of schools was selected based on having similar student outcomes before the intervention, and similar pre-intervention school characteristics. The selection of comparison schools was done in three different ways to verify that findings did not depend on which schools were chosen. **Appendix C** contains the details on the methodology, statistical analyses, and how the matched schools were selected. The tables and figures in this chapter are based on statistical models that used the nearest neighbor approach to choose comparison schools. The different methods of matching schools produced similar results to the nearest neighbor method. **Appendix C** provides the results of all three approaches. **Tables C.8 and C.9** show the results for elementary schools and **Tables C.14 and C.15** for high schools. These tables also present results from models with and without controlling for changes in student backgrounds.

The analyses examine the effects of all interventions together; there are insufficient numbers of schools in each type of intervention to make conclusions about the effects of any particular intervention. However, school-by-school results are provided in this chapter to show the variation in changes in student outcomes across schools.

In addition to controlling for observed characteristics in the analyses, sensitivity analyses were run to check for bias from unobserved covariates. **See Appendix C Table C.10** for the sensitivity analysis results.

Elementary Schools

We examined two outcomes for elementary schools, test scores in reading and test scores in math. Students in CPS take achievement tests each year in grades 3 through 8. For this analysis, students' scores were combined across the grades producing an average score for the entire school, regardless of which grade levels they served. Scores were converted into standard deviations from the system mean in each year and for each grade; thus, they can be interpreted as the degree to which students' scores were different from average in the system in that year. Standardizing within each year provides an automatic adjustment for any system wide trends that should not be attributed to the intervention, and for differences in tests, or scoring of tests, that may have occurred across the years.

Schools that were selected for intervention showed significantly lower test scores than other schools in the district during the years prior to intervention (see Figures 8 and 9). On average, their students' test scores were about half a standard deviation below the system average in reading and in math (0.46 standard deviations below average in reading, and 0.53 standard deviations below average in math). This is consistent with the intention of the intervention models to target very low-performing schools. Before the intervention took place, the comparison schools and the schools selected for intervention had very similar reading and math test scores and their trends were statistically no different from each other.

Elementary schools that went through reform made significant improvements in test scores compared with similar schools that did not; however, large improvements did not occur in the first year.
During the first year of the intervention, the schools undergoing intervention showed some improvements in reading and math test scores while the matched schools

FIGURE 8
Reading achievement in elementary schools was significantly better after the second year of intervention; after four years, the gap with the system average was reduced by almost half

Reading Scores in Treated and Comparison Schools

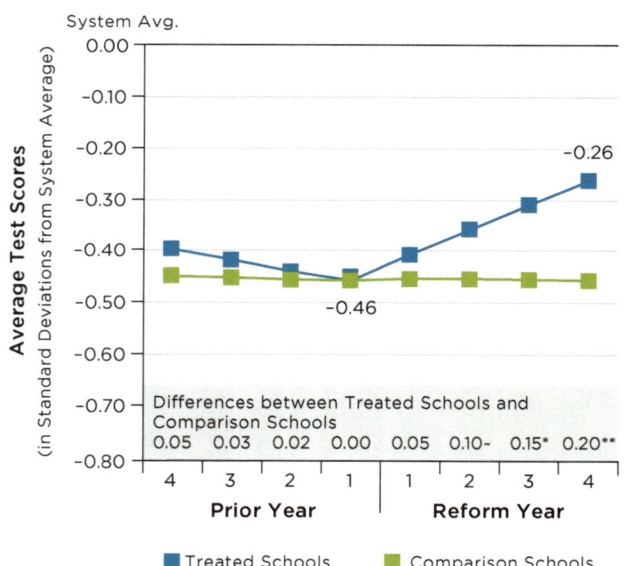

Note: These averages in the figure come from statistical models that chose comparison schools on the basis of the nearest neighbor approach and control for changes in students' background characteristics over time.

Significance: -p < 0.10, *p < 0.05, **p < 0.01, and ***p < 0.001

FIGURE 9
Math achievement at elementary schools was significantly better after the second year of intervention; after four years, the gap with the system average was cut by almost two-thirds

Mathematics Scores in Treated and Comparison Schools

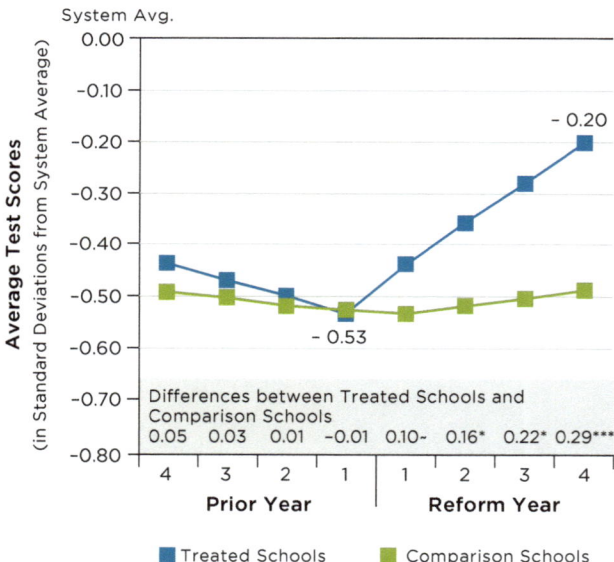

Note: These averages in the figure come from statistical models that chose comparison schools on the basis of the nearest neighbor approach and control for changes in students' background characteristics over time.

Significance: -p < 0.10, *p < 0.05, **p < 0.01, and ***p < 0.001

did not. The magnitude in the improvement in reading was 0.05 standard deviations and not statistically significant, in math the effect was larger, 0.10 standard deviations, and statistically different from the comparison group of schools.

During the subsequent three years, the intervention schools showed significantly higher growth in average test scores than the comparison schools. Reading scores were unchanged in comparison schools, but reading scores in intervention schools improved by 0.05 standard deviations more per year. This difference in growth is statistically significant. Thus, after three additional years of intervention, reading scores in intervention schools were 0.20 standard deviations higher than in the comparison schools. Math scores in intervention schools improved by 0.06 standard deviations each year, over and above the growth in the comparison schools. This difference in growth was statistically significant. Thus, after three additional years of intervention, math scores at intervention schools were 0.29 standard deviations higher than in the comparison schools.

After four years, treated schools were still below the system average, but improvements in test scores reduced the gap with the system average by almost half in reading and two-thirds in math.
The growth in test scores at the intervention schools diminished the gap between these schools and the system average by almost half in reading and by almost two-thirds in math at the end of four years of intervention.[41] In reading, average scores at intervention schools were 0.46 standard deviations below the system average the year prior to intervention. At the end of the fourth year, their scores were 0.26 standard deviations below the system average. In math, their scores were 0.53 standard deviations below the system before the intervention and 0.20 standard deviations below the system average after four years. The treated schools were still below the system average after four years, but significant improvements in test scores were evident after a few years.

It is important to note that the improvements reported in the first four years of intervention were beyond what would be expected from changes in the composition of students served by the school. Our analyses took into account changes in student characteristics and, even after controlling for students' background characteristics and prior achievement, the schools that underwent intervention showed significantly higher growth than the comparison schools. The effects without student controls are larger, given that some schools served a more advantaged student population (**see Appendix C**). Therefore, the estimates without student controls reflect improvements due to student population changes as well as real improvements in those schools. But even after controlling for the observable student characteristics, the effects are still positive and statistically significant, as discussed previously.

First year results were not consistent across schools, especially in reading, however, school-by-school growth was consistent in subsequent years.
Figures 10 and 11 show the first year effect and the average annual growth in the second, third and fourth year above the comparison group of schools for each of the treated schools. The first year effect in reading was quite variable across schools; most schools had modest effects with the exception of schools in the closure and restart that had large effects, still with a lot of variation among them. The average annual growth in reading in the next three years was remarkably consistent across schools. The average effect, as stated before, was 0.05 and the vast majority of schools were similar to the average.

In math, the first year results are much more consistent across schools, with most schools having similar results to the average effects shown previously. The overall first year effect was 0.10 standard deviations. Also the growth afterwards in years 2, 3, and 4 was, on average, 0.06 standard deviations and most schools had similar growth.

School-by-school results showed positive effects in most schools with a lot of consistency across schools in all the different interventions in this study. Most effects are very similar to the overall effect with only schools in the STSP model perhaps lagging behind other schools. Due to the limited number of schools, however, no definitive conclusions can be made about a particular model.

FIGURE 10

Improvement in reading scores was variable in the first year but more consistent in later years in almost all schools

Difference in Reading Growth at Elementary Schools That Underwent Reform Relative to the Average Growth at Comparison Schools

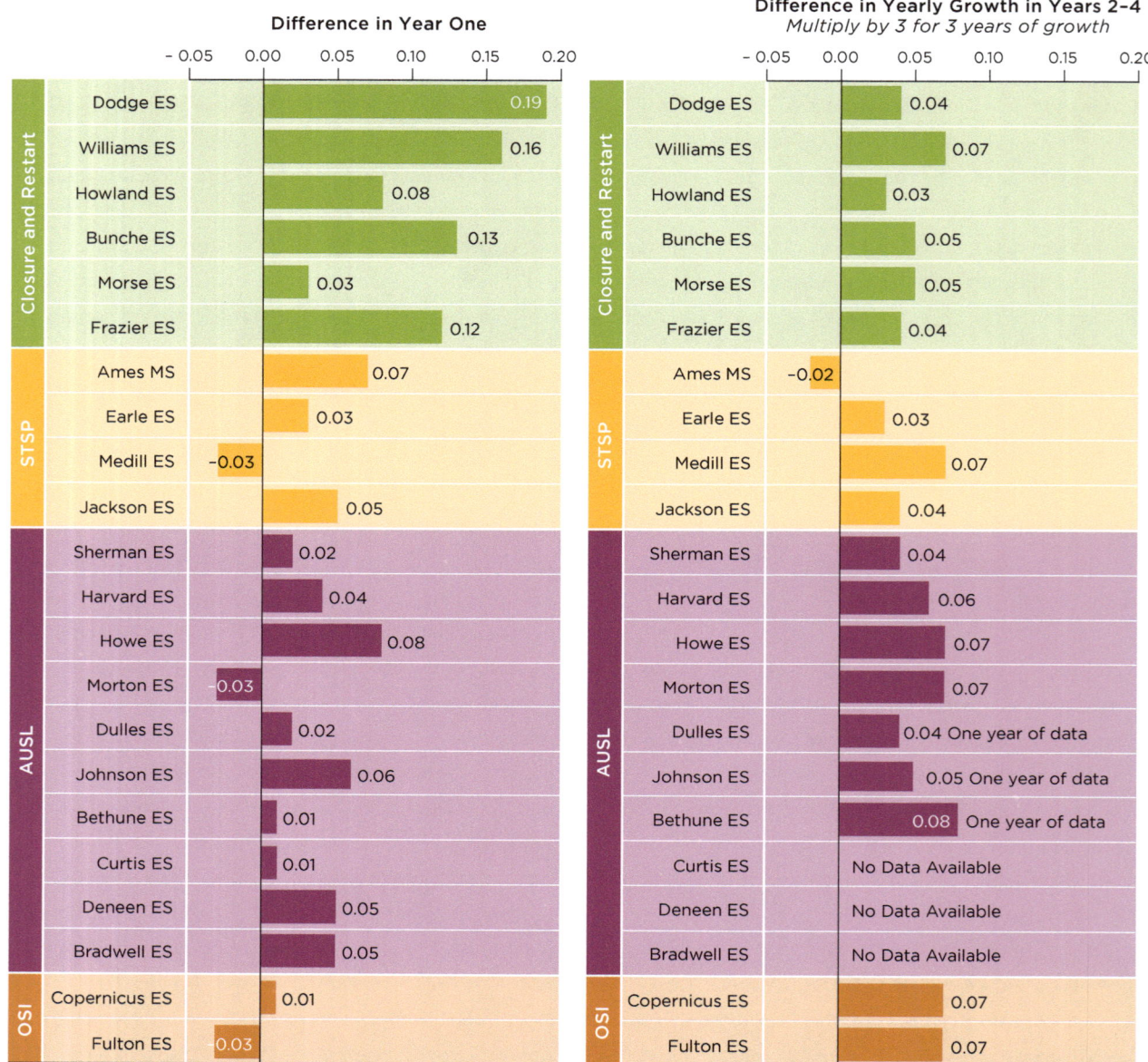

NOTE: These numbers come from statistical models that chose comparison schools on the basis of the nearest neighbor approach and control for changes in students' background characteristics over time. Units are in standard deviations and represent the first year effect and average post-intervention growth in years 2, 3, and 4 above the values of the comparison group of schools.

FIGURE 11

Improvement in math scores occurred at most elementary schools that underwent reform

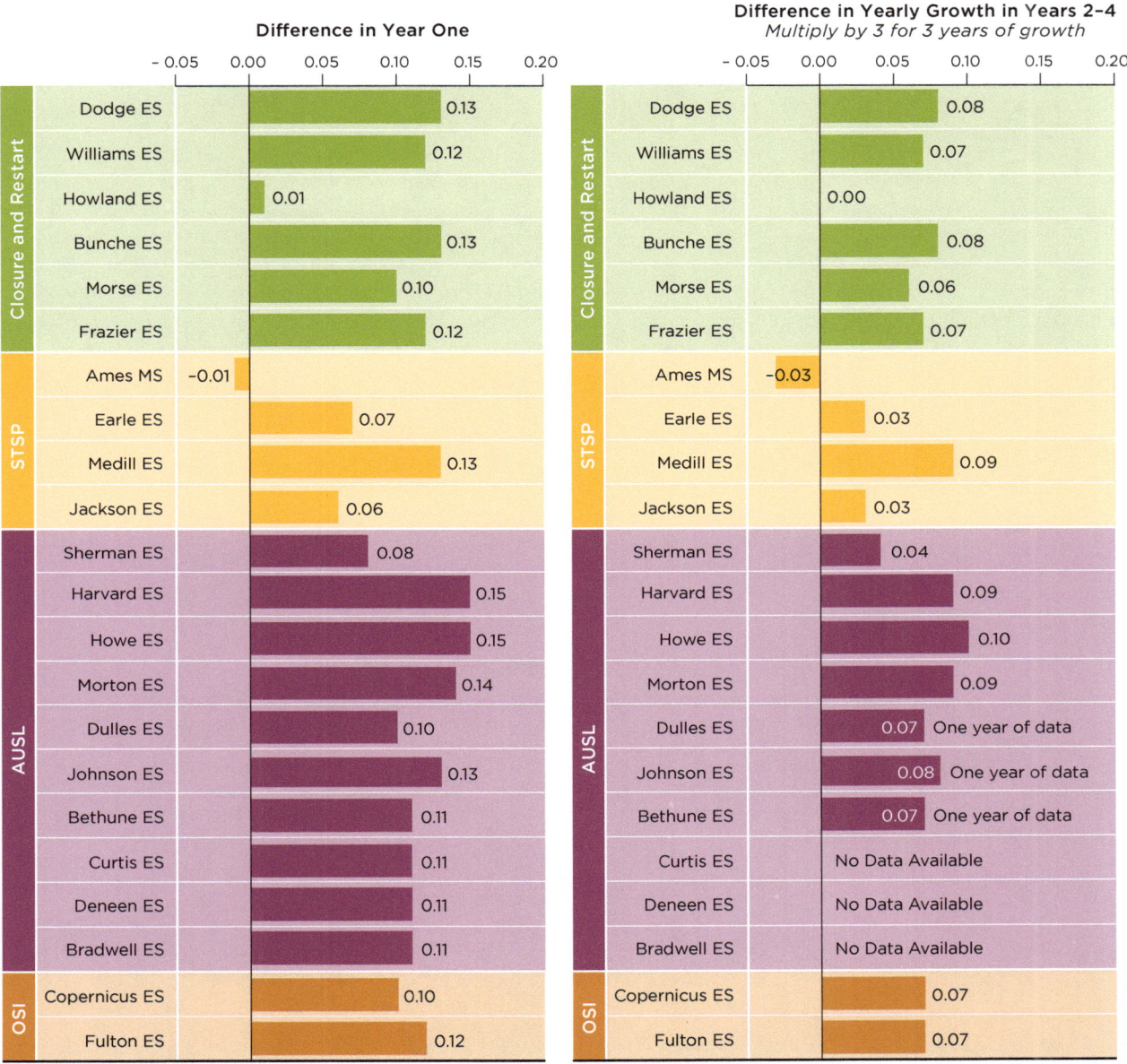

Difference in Mathematics Growth at Elementary Schools that Underwent Reform Relative to the Average Growth at Comparison Schools

NOTE: These numbers come from statistical models that chose comparison schools on the basis of the nearest neighbor approach and control for changes in students' background characteristics over time. Units are in standard deviations and represent the first year effect and average post-intervention growth in years 2, 3, and 4 above the values of the comparison group of schools.

A Different Way of Looking at the Elementary School Findings: A Simulation with ISAT Scores

Over time, elementary schools that underwent dramatic reforms in Chicago distanced themselves from other low-performing schools in terms of student achievement and substantially narrowed the gap with the district average. Because schools serve different grade levels, and the tests that were taken across the years changed, the analyses of changes in student achievement used metrics that allow us to compare different grades and tests. To put these findings in perspective, **Figures A and B** are created using the estimates from the regression models and the actual ISAT data from 2006 to 2011 for the district to simulate the trajectories for the groups of schools that underwent treatment and those similar schools that did not go through intervention. For simplicity, the simulation is done only for one grade, sixth grade, and for years during which many of the reforms occurred, 2006-11.

Figure A shows the actual trend for sixth graders in the district on their reading scale scores (blue line). It also shows the trajectory of reading scores for schools that underwent reform (red line) and the green line represents schools that started out with similar achievement levels and student demographics as the schools that underwent intervention but did not undergo reform. While the blue and green lines follow parallel trajectories, the red line makes a steeper climb. A similar pattern is evident for mathematic scores, shown in **Figure B**. All scores improved during this time period, but because of possible scoring inconsistencies from year-to-year on the ISAT, this does not necessarily represent real average system wide improvements in learning.[c] **The key comparison is the difference in the rate of improvement of treated schools (red line), relative to either the system average (blue line) or the schools that looked similar prior to reform (green line).** After four years, schools undergoing reform decreased the gap in scores by about 5 ISAT points in reading and about 9 ISAT points in math. Typical growth on the ISAT for sixth graders is about 13 points per year in reading and 16 in math. Thus, four years after turnaround, scores at intervention schools were higher in reading by the amount that a typical student learns in about three and a half months. The difference in math was more than half a year.

FIGURE A

After four years, treated schools narrowed the gap in READING by about 5 ISAT points

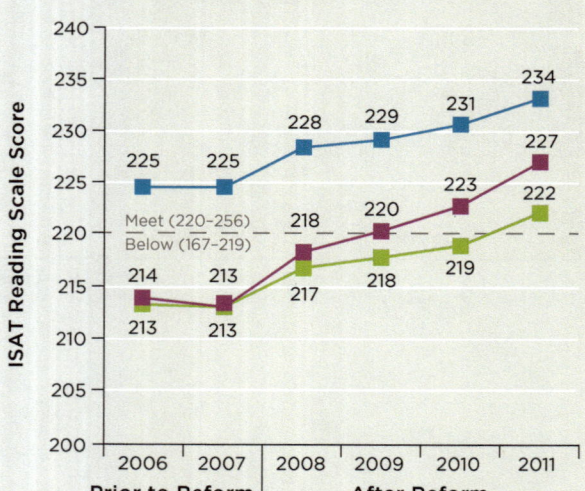

FIGURE B

After four years, treated schools narrowed the gap in MATH by about 9 ISAT points

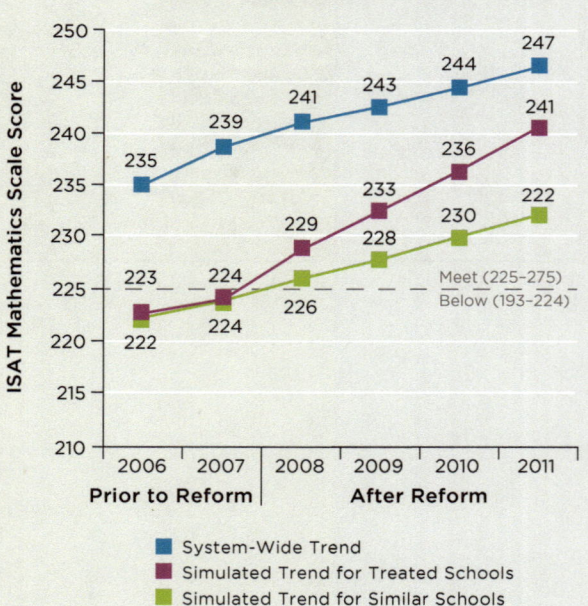

High Schools

Student absences in grades nine through 12 and on-track to graduate rates for students in ninth grade are the two indicators we studied for high schools. While we could not study test scores for high schools, these other indicators are important to study since they related to student graduation.

Student absences were recorded by CPS slightly differently in the years prior to 2007-08 than in the years after. In addition, only absences in the fall semester are available for one of the years, a year in which there was a change in the student information system. In order to make measures comparable, we converted each student's absence rate into standard deviations from the system mean for each fall semester. This makes the measure of absences consistent across all the years included in this study; they can be interpreted as the degree to which students' absences for the fall semester were different from the average in the system for that year. Standardizing within year also adjusts for any system-wide trends that should not be attributed to the interventions. The on-track to graduate variable was not standardized because it was measured in the same way for all years in the study.

Absences improved the first year after intervention, but that improvement was short lived.
Schools that were selected for intervention and their matched comparison schools had very similar absences prior to intervention. Absences for comparison schools were not significantly different from the treated schools just before intervention; nor were the trends in absences different in the three years prior to intervention (**see Figure 12**). These schools had significantly higher absences than other schools in the district. The year just prior to intervention the comparison schools were 0.48 standard deviations above the system average and the treated schools were 0.44 standard deviations above the system average.[42]

The first year after intervention treated schools reduced their absences to 0.20 standard deviations above average while comparison schools experienced an increase in their absences to 0.54 standard deviations above average. The difference between the two groups of schools is marginally statistically significant; however, in subsequent years, absences increased in the treated schools, and decreased in comparison schools, bringing the absences in these two groups of schools closer to each other over time.

On-track to graduate rates in treated schools did not improve at a different rate than at the comparison group of schools.
The on-track to graduate rates for intervention schools were not significantly different from the comparison schools in the intervention year, or in the three years prior to intervention (**see Figure 13**). On-track to graduate rates were improving in these schools in the years prior to intervention as they have been across the district.

The first year after intervention, both targeted and comparison schools made improvements in their on-track to graduate rates bigger than the annual growth prior to intervention, but the difference between targeted and comparison schools was not statistically significant. Increases in on-track to graduate rates continued after the first year for both groups of schools, with slightly larger increases in the treated schools, but the differences remained statistically insignificant.

All different methods of matching schools yielded very similar results with no significant differences between the treated schools and the comparison group of schools.

School-by-school results show a lot of variation across high schools, with more recent reform efforts showing some promising signs in on-track to graduate rates. **Figures 14 and 15** show the first year effect and the average annual growth in the second, third and fourth years above the comparison group of schools for each of the treated schools for absences and on-track to graduate indicator. The most salient feature in these graphs is the variability in the changes in student outcomes, both in the first year and the subsequent growth in both outcomes. Variability is evident among the schools in the sample that were part of the reconstitution model, and also among schools that were part of the more recent efforts in Chicago.

The first year effect on absences was quite large for a number of schools. The overall average effect was

FIGURE 12

High school absence rates were lower in the first year, on average, but not in subsequent years

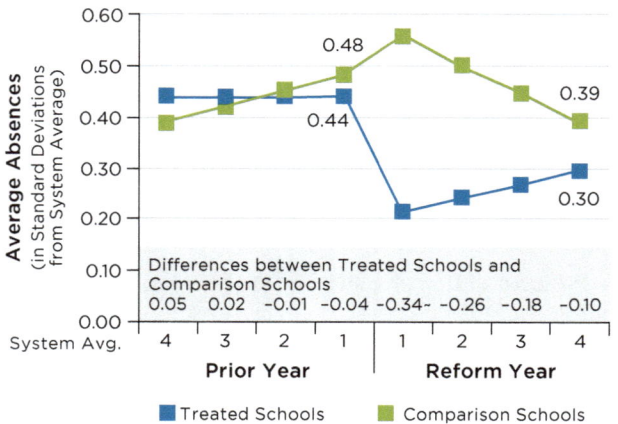

Note: These averages in the figure come from statistical models that chose comparison schools on the basis of the nearest neighbor approach and control for changes in students' background characteristics over time.

Significance: -p < 0.10, *p < 0.05, **p < 0.01, and ***p < 0.001

FIGURE 13

Ninth grade on-track rates in treated schools were not different from comparison schools

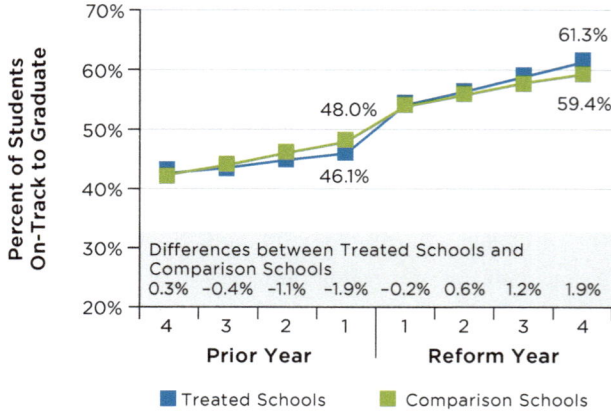

Note: These averages come from statistical models that chose comparison schools on the basis of the nearest neighbor approach and control for changes in students' background characteristics over time. There are minor differences between this graph and the graph in the summary report because of a mistake in the calculations of on-track numbers from the model.

Significance: -p < 0.10, *p < 0.05, **p < 0.01, and ***p < 0.001

FIGURE 14

There was large variation across high schools in improvements in absence rates

Differences in Absences at High Schools that Underwent Reform Relative to Comparison Schools

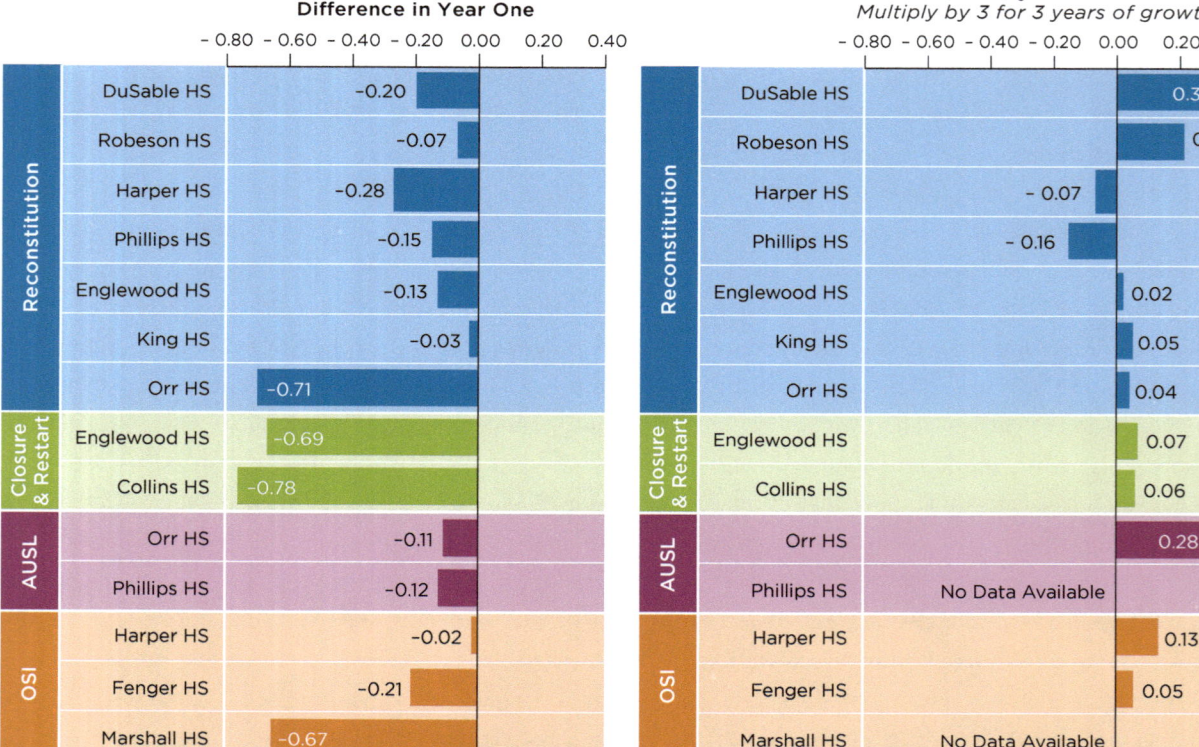

NOTE: These numbers come from statistical models that chose comparison schools on the basis of the nearest neighbor approach and control for changes in students' background characteristics over time. Units are in standard deviations and represent the first year effect and average post-intervention growth in years 2, 3, and 4 above the values of the comparison group of schools.

FIGURE 15

Recent reform efforts showed more improvements in on-track rates than earlier efforts

Differences in On-Track Rates at High Schools that Underwent Reform Relative to Comparison Schools

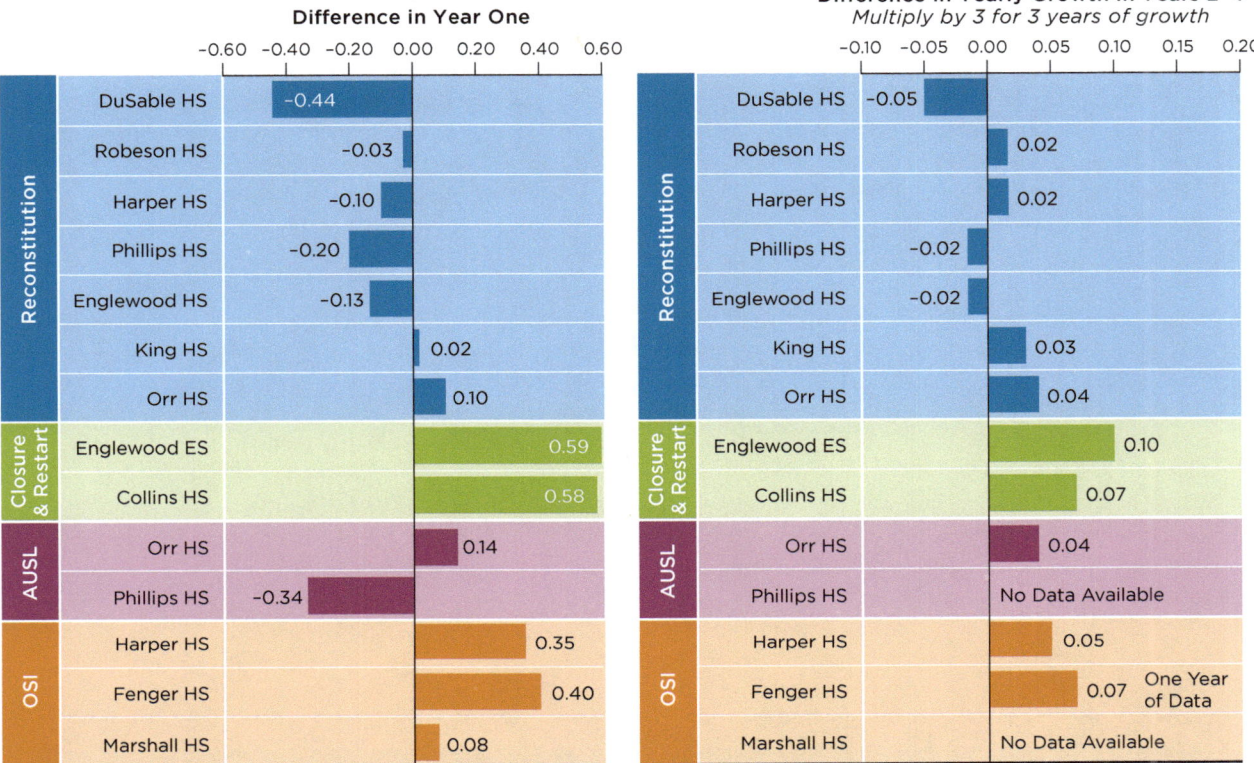

NOTE: These numbers come from statistical models that chose comparison schools on the basis of the nearest neighbor approach and control for changes in students' background characteristics over time. Units are in logits and represent the first year effect and average post-intervention growth in years 2, 3, and 4 above the values of the comparison group of schools.

a decrease of 0.34 standard deviations, with four of the schools showing changes well beyond that. These four schools seemed to be driving the average change described previously. The effect on absences in the next three years was, however, in the opposite direction—with increasing absences in most schools, even those with declining absences in the first year.

The effect on on-track to graduate rates are quite variable among schools, with most of the schools in the recent reforms showing more positive changes than most of the reconstituted schools. The first year results were positive for the vast majority of the schools under the most recent interventions with further improvements in subsequent years. This is over and above an increase in on-track rates that was occurring system-wide.

Limitations and Considerations for Interpreting the Results

The conclusions from this study are limited by several factors. The schools CPS selected for intervention were not chosen at random; they were chosen from among a larger pool of low-performing schools. We used careful matching techniques to identify comparison groups of similar schools, on the basis of the available observed data. There is still the possibility, however, that the selected intervention schools differ from the comparison schools in ways not captured by the propensity matching methods.

It is also possible that the characteristics of students in intervention schools differ from those in comparison schools in ways other than the observed characteristics that the model accounted for. For example, students in the intervention schools, especially those with higher prior scores, could have been on a faster learning trajectory or had more supportive parents, leading to a higher growth for these students.

Further, it is plausible that the comparison schools might have been affected indirectly by the intervention efforts. Specifically, comparison schools may have believed that they were targeted for future intervention, because the treatment schools were selected on the basis of their achievement levels and because the achievement levels of the comparison schools were similar to those in the treatment schools. This belief may, in turn, have led to changes in achievement levels. For high schools, our caliper-based matching method failed to find adequate comparison schools for more than half the intervention schools. This highlights the fact the schools chosen for intervention were among the lowest-performing schools in the district, with unique demographic characteristics. Using propensity methods highlighted the lack of overlap between treatment and control schools in our high school sample. Yet the lack of overlap can lead to imprecise estimates and introduce biases such as regression to the mean. Therefore the model estimates for high schools must be interpreted with caution.

Although fidelity to implementation greatly influences the effects of intervention, examining the degree to which the CPS reform interventions actually were carried out and implemented is beyond the scope of this study. Understanding fidelity would provide useful insight into why some schools might have better outcomes than others. Rather, this study focused specifically on the overall changes over time in schools selected for intervention by CPS, which is an important contribution even without information on implementation. Thus, results should be interpreted as the general trend across all intervention schools.

This study focused on a subset of reform interventions put forth by CPS during the past 15 years rather than one specific, well-defined intervention. These interventions share the general goal of rapidly reforming and turning around low-performing schools, but have different approaches and requirements. We did not attempt to examine or characterize any differences in the effects on student outcomes across the interventions. The intent of the study was to examine whether any changes over time were associated with this set of substantive, district-led reform interventions.

CHAPTER 5

Interpretive Summary

Between 1997 and 2010, 36 CPS schools were identified as chronically low performing and underwent reforms that share key elements of the school improvement models currently promoted by the U.S. Department of Education—elements such as replacement of leadership, staff, and school governance or attendance rules.

While there has been substantial national attention drawn to some of the schools as successful models of the federal government strategies for low-performing schools, there have been questions as to what actually occurred at the schools and how they correspond to current federal definitions of reform.

One complicating factor is knowing which strategy was actually used at which school and what happened to the teaching staff with reform. The federal guidelines came out years after most of these Chicago schools had gone through intervention; therefore, CPS reform labels do not correspond to the current federal definitions, even though much of the terminology appears to be the same. For example, "turnaround" in Chicago is used to refer to two different models.

Most of the interventions described here included a change in staff as one of their primary levers of reform. Changing the entire staff is a politically difficult move for the district. It also requires substantial effort to find qualified replacement staff. Thus, it is important to know what types of changes in staffing actually occurred with the intervention—who was actually teaching in these schools before and after reform. While a new staff might make it easier to enact substantial changes in school practice, difficulties in quickly staffing a new school might bring a new set of problems.

There are also concerns that public statements about improved performance in some of the schools might be biased in some way—either because the schools served different types of students after reform than before, or because the metrics used to measure improvement are misleading. In Chicago, the tests that are given to students have changed over time, and the equivalence of the year-to-year scores on state tests has been questioned, making it very difficult to compare current and past performance using publicly reported statistics.[43]

An additional area of concern is that, despite often being touted as means to bring about accelerated improvement in very low-performing schools, these were new initiatives when they were implemented and there is a lack of research on their effectiveness. It is only now, years after implementation, that adequate data exist to analyze the changes in outcomes of the different turnaround models.

With interventions that are as politically controversial as these, a lack of clear, valid information can aggravate conflict among the many constituents in the educational community because no one is sure of what has actually happened. The data presented here show that the picture is complex and can support many interpretations—proponents of the policy can point to success, while opponents can point to concerns. The data in this report provide a factual base for discussing the actual benefits and problems associated with these types of reform.

Some schools served a different population of students who tended to be more advantaged, but most schools saw the same students reenrolling after reform; most schools served fewer students after reform.
Whether the schools served the same students after reform as before, reform is not only an issue for judging whether changes in student outcomes were a result of improving schools but also an issue of social justice in the communities being served. Proponents of dramatic reform efforts emphasize the critical importance of improving the educational experience of students who are not being served well. Yet, community groups in Chicago often oppose these efforts out of concern that the reforms will push neighborhood students from their neighborhood school. This research suggests that the concerns of these critics are valid for one type of reform model but not for the others.

With the exception of the schools that closed and reopened, most schools reenrolled students who had been in the schools prior to the intervention, and the types of students served by the schools were similar before and after the intervention in terms of race/ethnicity, socioeconomic status, the percentage of students identified for special education services, and the degree to which schools served students from the neighborhood around the school. Thus, for most models, there is no credence to claims that improvements in student outcomes were simply a result of serving more advantaged students. In fact, in subsequent years, more students returned year-to-year in these schools than in the years prior to reform. These schools seemed to do a better job of holding onto their students (i.e., reducing mobility) and continued to serve students from their local community.

The Closure and Restart model, however, introduced substantial changes to the student composition in these schools, with reenrollment rates falling below 50 percent of the original students. These schools were closed for an academic year or more and used a lottery admission process when they reopened. These features likely deterred or prevented students from reenrolling. After reopening, the Closure and Restart schools also tended to serve more economically advantaged students, students of higher initial abilities, and fewer special education students. Thus, schools that were closed and restarted were less likely to serve their original communities, or even students with characteristics similar to those who were previously served by the school. These changes also may help explain the student outcomes, which were substantially higher after reform. Claims have been made about the success of some of these schools without taking into consideration which students they were serving.

Intervention schools, regardless of model, served fewer students after reform than before. Under all of the models, the size of the schools declined with intervention; 27 out of 36 schools served fewer students per grade during the first year of intervention, with five schools serving at least one quarter fewer students. Four of the schools with the largest declines in enrollment followed the Closure and Restart model. This structural change in school size also could have affected the operation of the school and the likelihood of success. There is research that suggests small schools are easier to reform, and that students show better behavior and are less likely to dropout.[44] However, despite the decline in size of schools under-going reform, not many of these schools would be considered small schools (which tend to be defined as no more than 350 students for elementary schools and 500 students for high schools).

It is difficult to restaff a school in one year; the teaching staff was less experienced in most schools after reform, and there was a shift in teachers' racial composition.
All but one of CPS's turnaround initiatives called for major personnel changes in teaching staff. Schools under the Reconstitution model had little time to restaff; the interventions were implemented in a brief time over the summer of 1997. As a result, changes to personnel in these schools were not substantial, and approximately half of the original teachers were rehired. In contrast, schools under the Closure and Restart model remained closed for a full academic year or more before reopening, resulting in a complete change in staff at most schools. Schools in the AUSL and OSI models also rehired just a small fraction of their original teaching force, ranging between 0 and 23.5 percent from school to school.

Because so many new teachers were hired, it is not surprising that there was a shift in the composition of teachers at most schools. Teachers in the schools after the intervention were younger, had less experience, and were more likely to have provisional certification compared to teachers in the same schools before the intervention. Previous research has shown that novice teachers may present some challenges for schools.[45] It takes a few years for teachers to hone their craft, and novice teachers need more support than more seasoned teachers to develop their teaching skills. Moreover, new teachers are more likely to leave the profession within five years. These two facts might present future challenges for these schools to support and retain their teacher workforce.

District-wide, the teaching workforce has become increasingly white and less African American, and this trend accelerated in these schools in the year they re-hired most of their staff. This is a concern since most of the schools that have been reformed almost exclusively serve African American students. To the extent that African American teachers may more easily serve as role models for African American children, may have a better understanding of family and community issues, or may be perceived as having a better understanding of the neighborhood than young white teachers, the shift in teacher racial characteristics may also be a detriment for the schools.

Elementary schools did not immediately "turn around" student achievement with the intervention, but they improved significantly more than other schools over time—a rare occurrence among schools most in need of improvement.

Reading and math scores in elementary schools that underwent turnaround reforms improved gradually over the first four years of intervention. Improvements were not observed immediately in the first year, at least in reading, and performance remained lower than the district average in both subjects. However, the observed improvements in test scores at the end of four years reduced the gap between these schools and the district average by almost half in reading and by almost two-thirds in math.

If the post-intervention trends were extrapolated out for more years at the observed rate, scores in the intervention schools would reach the system average in five more years (nine total years of intervention) in reading and in three more years (seven total years of intervention) in math. This assumes that they continue to improve at the same rate.

The slow growth in achievement might be disappointing for those who expected turnarounds to dramatically close the achievement gap between low- and high-performing schools in the space of one or two years. These highly disruptive reforms are often justified with arguments that students cannot wait for their schools to show incremental improvements. On the other hand, these dramatic reform efforts in Chicago did accelerate learning at a significantly faster rate than the district average. In fact, the rate of gains made by these previously chronically underperforming schools was higher than virtually every other school in the city between 2001 and 2009—the period of time studied for a previous report on trends in Chicago.[46] Moreover, this prior study showed that schools most in need of improvement were the least likely to improve throughout three eras of different reforms in Chicago. To the extent that these schools were located in neighborhoods with low social capital and high crime, these improvements are more laudable since schools in these circumstances have proven time and time again to be the most impervious to reform. An earlier study of Chicago school improvement from 1990-1996 showed that schools located in neighborhoods with high crime rates and low social capital needed to have exceptionally strong organizational structures to show strong improvements in student achievement, compared to schools serving more advantaged students.[47]

These types of reforms showed less success at the high school level than at the elementary level, although further research is needed.

High schools that went through turnaround reforms did not show sustained and significant improvements in absences or on-track to graduate rates over matched comparison schools, but it is important to note that Reconstituted schools comprise the majority of turnaround high schools studied in this report. Some of these schools were again targeted for subsequent models of turnaround reforms in later years, suggesting that some of these schools were still low performing even after being reconstituted. There is insufficient data on the more recent models of turnaround reforms for high schools to conclusively evaluate the success of the new models separately from the old ones. Individual schools, however, do show improvements over their past performance, and compared to other low-performing schools. These are promising, though not conclusive, signs for newer attempts at reform.

Similar results to those in Chicago have emerged from Philadelphia's Renaissance Initiative, where 13 persistently low-performing schools were targeted for intervention in 2010.[48] In Philadelphia, six schools remained under the supervision of the district and seven were managed by charter organizations. Achievement and attendance improved in the elementary schools in the first year of intervention, but there were no changes to those outcomes in the two high schools. When coupled with the findings in Chicago, this provides additional, suggestive evidence that such reforms may be more difficult to implement in high schools. It is also possible, however, that it simply takes more time to see improvements in high school outcomes. Graduation and college-going rates, for example, cannot be studied until four or more years after reforms have taken place. It is possible that improvements in these other outcomes will be seen in the future.

Beyond changing school staff, the emphasis on improving school organization in the newer models is supported by research on schools that have successfully turned around student performance. Other studies have suggested that successful efforts to turn around low-performing schools have done so by building the organizational strength of the school over time, using staff changes as just one of many mechanisms to improve school climate and instruction. A list of recommendations compiled in the Institute of Education Sciences' Practice Guide on School Turnaround[49], based on case studies of schools that showed substantial improvement, starts with establishing strong leadership focused on improving school climate and instruction, strengthening partnerships across school communities, monitoring instruction, addressing discipline, and building distributed leadership among teachers in the school. The second recommendation is to maintain a consistent focus on improving instruction by having staff collaborate around data to analyze school policies and learning conditions. The third recommendation is to pursue quick wins that target critical but immediately addressable problems, including student discipline and safety, conflict in the school community, and school beautification. The final recommendation is to build a committed staff that is dedicated to school improvement through collaboration. None of the successful schools highlighted in the IES practice guide changed its entire staff, but all of them replaced teachers who did not share a commitment to change.

Similar conclusions about turning around school performance come from a study of middle schools in New York in which schools that made substantial progress from 2006 to 2010 were compared to similar schools that showed no progress.[50] This study suggested a need for aligning needs, goals, and actions, creating a positive work environment and addressing student discipline and safety in school as essential conditions for improving teaching and learning. These schools worked on developing their teachers, creating small learning communities, targeting student sub-populations, and using data to inform instruction as a way to improve teaching and learning. Eventually, academic improvements emerged when principals and teachers collaborated to create and maintain these conditions and worked together on the strategies to improve learning in their schools.

The importance of building a robust school organization is further highlighted in a research study by CCSR examining 100 elementary schools that made significant progress over a seven-year period—and 100 more that did not. The research found that schools strong on at least three of five essential elements—effective leaders, collaborative teachers, strong family and community ties, ambitious instruction, and safe and orderly learning climate—were 10 times more likely to improve and 30 times less likely to stagnate than those that were weak in at least three areas.[51] Perhaps it is not surprising, then, that the recent reform models, OSI and AUSL—both of which have explicit blueprints for reform focused on building the organizational strength of schools—achieved consistent improvement in most of the elementary schools they managed.

Building a vibrant school organization takes time, effort, and resources. Recent initiatives in Chicago to rapidly turn around performance have recognized the value of school organization and have put resources and efforts into building strong schools, as well as replacing staff. This study suggests that these efforts have paid off, but we cannot determine whether the improvements came about because of the change in staff, an increase in resources, the concerted efforts to strengthen the schools as organizations, or the combination of all factors together. It does suggest that turning around chronically low-performing schools is a process rather than an event. It does not occur immediately when staff or leadership or governance structures are replaced, but it can occur when strategically focused effort and resources are sustained over time.

These schools started out with extremely low levels of student performance and presented significant barriers to reform. As our prior study showed, these schools had a negligible probability of improving.[52] From this perspective, this study provides promising evidence about efforts to improve chronically low-performing schools—showing improvements in schools that historically have been most impervious to reform.

Issues for Future Research

Which Aspects of Reform Are Most Critical?

Because of the small number of schools that have gone through each intervention model, this project had insufficient cases to be able to identify the characteristics of the intervention models that have been most successful. As more cities engage in such reform, future research might combine information from those places to gain a more comprehensive understanding of the effects of these models. There was considerable variation in the trends across schools that underwent intervention, ranging from schools that showed no improvement to one school that came close to approaching the system mean in terms of student achievement. These differences may have been a result of fidelity to intervention or the specific circumstances of the individual schools (e.g., a particularly effective or ineffective leader), or they might have resulted from particular aspects of the intervention models. Future research might investigate the factors that made these interventions most likely to show substantial improvements in students' achievement.

Long-Term Impacts of Turnaround Reform

Besides encompassing a larger number of schools, future studies also might gauge long-term effects of these intervention models on student achievement beyond the first four years, particularly if attention and resources from the district start to fade. Although the short-term gains in elementary schools are significant, achievement in the schools that underwent intervention remained well below the system average. Future studies might be able to discern whether these schools eventually reached average achievement levels, the gains observed in the first few years dissipated, or the scores fell back to earlier levels.

References

Allensworth, E.M., and Easton, J.Q. (with Chaplin, D.). (2005)
The on-track indicator as a predictor of high school graduation. Chicago: Consortium on Chicago School Research.

Allensworth, E.M., and Easton, J.Q. (2007)
What matters for staying on-track and graduating in Chicago public schools. Chicago: Consortium on Chicago School Research.

Austin, P.C. (2011)
Optimal caliper widths for propensity-score matching when estimating differences in means and differences in proportions in observational studies. *Pharmaceutical Statistics, 10*(2):150-161.

Bryk, A.S., Bender Sebring, P., Allensworth, E.M., Luppescu, S., and Easton, J.Q. (2010)
Organizing schools for improvement: Lessons from Chicago. Chicago: University of Chicago Press.

Calkins, A., Guenther, W., Belfiore, G., and Lash, D. (2007)
The turnaround challenge: Why America's best opportunity to dramatically improve student achievement lies in our worst-performing schools. Boston, MA: Mass Insight. Retrieved April 28, 2011, from http://www.massinsight.org/publications/turnaround/51/file/1/pubs/2010.04/15/TheTurnaroundChallenge_Main.

Charles A. Dana Center. (2001)
Opening doors: Promising lessons from five Texas high schools. Austin: University of Texas at Austin, Charles A. Dana Center. Retrieved April 28, 2011, from http://www.utdanacenter.org/downloads/products/openingdoors/hscrosscase.pdf.

Chicago Public Schools. (1999)
Reengineering. Chicago, IL: Author. Unpublished document.

Chicago Public Schools. (2009a)
Phased school support. Chicago, IL: Author. Unpublished document

Chicago Public Schools. (2009b)
Turning around comprehensive high schools: Implementation of CPS turnaround model at the high school level. Chicago: Author. Unpublished document.

Chicago Public Schools. (2010)
Renaissance 2010 (Web page). Retrieved April 28, 2011, from http://www.ren2010.cps.k12.il.us.

Cotton, K. (1996)
School size, school climate, and student performance. Close-up #20. Portland, OR: Northwest Regional Educational Laboratory.

de la Torre, M., and Gwynne, J. (2009)
When schools close: Effects on displaced students in Chicago Public Schools. Chicago: University of Chicago, Consortium on Chicago School Research.

Finnigan, K., and O'Day, J. (with Wakelyn, D.). (2003)
External support to schools on probation: Getting a leg up? Chicago: University of Chicago, Consortium on Chicago School Research.

Gladden, R. (1998)
The small school movement: A review of the literature. In M. Fine and J.I. Somerville (Eds.), *Small schools, big imaginations: A creative look at urban public schools.* Chicago: Cross City Campaign for Urban School Reform.

Gold, E., Norton, M., Good, D., and Levin, S. (2012)
Philadelphia's Renaissance School Initiative: 18 Month Interim Report. Philadelphia, PA: Research for Action. Retrieved February 22, 2012, from http://www.research-foraction.org/wp-content/uploads/2012/02/RFA-Renaissance-Schools-18-Month-Report.pdf.

Haviland, A., Nagin, D.S., and Rosenbaum, P.R. (2007)
Combining propensity score matching and group-based trajectory analysis in an observational study. *Psychological Methods, 12*(3), 247-267.

Herman, R., Dawson, P., Dee, T., Greene, J., Maynard, R., Redding, S., et al. (2008)
Turning around chronically low-performing schools (IES practice guide, NCEE #2008-4020). Washington, DC: U. S. Department of Education, Institute of Education Sciences, National Center for Education Evaluation and Regional Assistance. Retrieved April 28, 2011, from http://ies.ed.gov/ncee/wwc/pdf/practiceguides/Turnaround_pg_04181.pdf.

Hess, G.A. (2003)
Reconstitution—three years later: Monitoring the effect of sanctions on Chicago high schools. *Education and Urban Society, 35*(3), 300-327.

Johnson, S.M., Birkeland, S.E., Donaldson, M.L., Kardos, S.M., Kauffman, D., Liu, E., and Peske, H.G. (2004)
Finders and keepers: Helping new teachers survive and thrive in our schools. San Francisco, CA: Jossey-Bass.

Kahne, J.E., Sporte, S., and de la Torre, M. with Easton, J.Q. (2006)
Small Schools on a Larger Scale: The First Three Years of the Chicago High School Redesign Initiative. Chicago: University of Chicago, Consortium on Chicago School Research.

Kowal, J.M., and Hassel, E.A. (2005)
Turnarounds with new leaders and staff (School restructuring options under No Child Left Behind: What works when? Series). Washington, DC: The Center for Comprehensive School Reform and Improvement. Retrieved April 28, 2011, from http://www.centerforcsri.org/pubs/restructuring/KnowledgeIssues4Turnaround.pdf.

Luppescu, S., Allensworth, E., Moore, P., de la Torre, M., Murphy, J., with Jagesic, S. (2011)
Trends in Chicago's Schools Across Three Eras of Reform: Full Report. Chicago, IL: Consortium on Chicago School Research.

Meyers, C.V., and Murphy, J. (2008)
Turning around failing schools: An analysis. *Journal of School Leadership, 17*(5), 631-659.

Morgan, S.L., and Harding, D.J. (2006)
Matching estimators of causal effects: Prospects and pitfalls in theory and practice. *Sociological Methods and Research, 35*(3), 3-60.

Murphy, J., and Meyers, C.V. (2008)
Turning around failing schools: Leadership lessons from the organizational sciences. Thousand Oaks, CA: Corwin Press.

Partnership for Leaders in Education. (2010)
University of Virginia School Turnaround Specialist Program. Charlottesville: University of Virginia, Partnership for Leaders in Education. Retrieved April 28, 2011, from http://www.darden.virginia.edu/web/Darden-Curry-PLE/UVA-School-Turnaround/Program/.

Picucci, A.C., Brownson A., Kahlet, R., and Sobel, A. (2002)
Driven to succeed: High-performing, high-poverty, turnaround middle schools: Vol. 2. Case studies. Austin: University of Texas at Austin, Charles A. Dana Center. Retrieved April 28, 2011, from http://www.utdanacenter.org/downloads/products/driven/ms_vol2.pdf.

Public Impact. (2008)
Chicago school turnarounds: Final report. Chicago: Chicago Public Education Fund. Unpublished document.

Race to the Top Fund: Final Rule, 74 Fed. Reg. 58462 (2009)
Retrieved April 28, 2011, from http://www2.ed.gov/legislation/FedRegister/finrule/2009-4/111809a.pdf.

Raudenbush, S.W. (2009)
Adaptive centering with random effects: An alternative to the fixed effects model for studying time-varying treatments in school settings. *Journal of Education, Finance and Policy, 4*(4), 468-491.

Rhim, L.M., Kowal, J.M., Hassel, B.C., and Hassel E.A. (2007)
School turnarounds: A review of the cross-sector evidence on dramatic organizational improvement. Lincoln, IL: Center on Innovation & Improvement. Retrieved April 28, 2011, from http://www.centerii.org/survey/downloads/Turnarounds-Color.pdf.

Rosenbaum, P.R. (2002)
Observational studies. New York, NY: Springer.

Sporte, S. and de la Torre, M. (2010)
Chicago High School Redesign Initiative: Schools, Students, and Outcomes. Chicago: University of Chicago, Consortium on Chicago School Research.

U.S. Department of Education. (2009)
Obama administration announces historic opportunity to turn around nation's lowest-achieving public schools. Washington, DC: Author. Retrieved April 28, 2011, from http://www.ed.gov/news/pressreleases/2009/08/08262009.html.

U.S. Department of Education. (2010)
Achieving dramatic school improvement: An exploratory study. Washington, DC: Author. Retrieved April 28, 2011, from http://www.wested.org/online_pubs/dramatic-improvement-report.pdf.

Villavicencio, A., and Grayman, J. (2012)
Learning from "Turnaround" Middle Schools: Strategies for Success. New York, NY: Research Alliance for New York City Schools. Retrieved February 22, 2012, from http://steinhardt.nyu.edu/scmsAdmin/media/users/jnw216/RANYCS/WebDocs/RANYCS-MiddleSchoolTurnaround-Report-20120214.pdf.

Wolk, R. (1998)
Strategies for fixing failing public schools. *Education Week* (online edition). Retrieved April 28, 2011, from http://www.edweek.org/ew/articles/1998/11/18/12pew.h18.html.

Wong, K.K. (2000)
Big change questions: Chicago school reform: From decentralization to integrated governance. *Journal of Educational Change, 1*(1), 95-103.

Appendix A
Description of Low-Performing Schools that Underwent Intervention

This appendix presents a brief description of the schools that the district identified over the years as chronically low-performing schools. In the case where a school was replaced by another, the new name and grade structure of the school is provided as well. All schools prior to intervention were traditional neighborhood schools where students living in proximity were assigned to attend. This might have changed after intervention and when that is the case, it is reflected in the columns under school governance after intervention and attendance rules. We have also collected information on other changes and supports that might have taken place after the intervention in the last column of **Table A.1**.

A few other schools were identified by the district as chronic low-performing schools but are not included in our study. These were schools that closed and where no other schools were opened in that building or where the schools that reopened in the building did not serve any of the same grade levels. In these circumstances, the schools could not be included in the analyses because there is nothing to compare before and after reform. **Table A.2** lists the set of low-performing schools not included in the study.

TABLE A.1

Low-performing schools that underwent intervention

Timing of Intervention	Original School Name	New School Name	Grades Served Prior to Intervention	Grades Served First Year after Intervention (at full capacity)	School Governance after Intervention	Attendance Rules	Later Changes and Other Supports
Reconstitution Model							
Summer 1997	DuSable HS	—	9-12	9-12	Traditional		Went through intervention in fall 2000. Closed at the end of 2005-06.
Summer 1997	Robeson HS	—	9-12	9-12	Traditional		Reengineered in fall 1999. IDS intervention starting in fall 2008.
Summer 1997	Harper HS	—	9-12	9-12	Traditional		Reengineered in fall 1999. Became a Turnaround School supported by the Office of Improvement in fall 2008. Instructional Development System (IDS) intervention starting in fall 2008.
Summer 1997	Phillips HS	—	9-12	9-12	Traditional		Reengineered in fall 1999. IDS intervention starting in fall 2006. Turnaround by AUSL in fall 2010.
Summer 1997	Englewood HS	—	9-12	9-12	Traditional		Reengineered in fall 1999. Closed at the end of 2007-08.
Summer 1997	King HS	—	9-12	9-12	Traditional		Began a transition to become a selective enrollment school by not enrolling freshmen in fall 1999.
Summer 1997	Orr HS	—	9-12	9-12	Traditional		Went through intervention in fall 2000. Closed at the end of 2003-04. Three high schools that replaced Orr were turned around by AUSL in fall 2008. IDS intervention starting in fall 2008.
Closure and Restart Model							
Closed at the end of 2001-02; reopened in fall 2003.	Dodge ES	Dodge Renaissance Academy	K-8	K-8 (K-8)	Contract	Accepts students citywide through random lottery.	Starting in fall 2003, it became a Professional Development School for AUSL.
Closed at the end of 2001-02; reopened in fall 2003 as four separate schools (one served high school grades).	Williams ES	Williams Multiplex	K-8	K-3 (K-5)	Contract	Accepts students citywide through random lottery.	
		Williams Prep Academy		4-8 (6-8)	Contract	Accepts students citywide through random lottery.	
		KIPP Chicago Youth Village Academy		4-5 (5-7)	Contract	Accepts students citywide through random lottery.	Closed at the end of 2005-06. The KIPP foundation believed their model was best suited to the charter school environment.
Closed at the end of 2004-05; reopened in fall 2006.	Howland ES	Catalyst Charter—Howland	K-8	4-5 (K-8)	Charter	Accepts students citywide through random lottery.	Renaissance 2010 School
Closed at the end of 2004-05; reopened in fall 2006.	Bunche ES	Providence Englewood Charter—Bunche	K-8	K-5 (K-8)	Charter	Accepts students citywide through random lottery.	Renaissance 2010 School
Stopped taking freshmen in fall 2005 and closed at the end of 2007-08; two new schools opened up, one in fall 2006 and the other in fall 2007.	Englewood HS	Urban Prep Academy for Young Men Charter—Englewood	9-12	9 (9-12)	Charter	Accepts students citywide through random lottery.	Renaissance 2010 School
		TEAM Englewood		9 (9-12)	Performance	Accepts students citywide through random lottery.	Renaissance 2010 School
Closed at the end of 2005-06; reopened in fall 2007.	Morse ES	Polaris Charter Academy	K-8	K-2 (K-8)	Charter	Accepts students citywide through random lottery.	Renaissance 2010 School
Closed at the end of 2005-06; reopened in fall 2007.	Frazier ES	Frazier International Magnet	K-8	K-5 (K-8)	Performance	Accepts students citywide through random lottery.	Renaissance 2010 School
		Frazier Preparatory Academy		K-5 (K-8)	Contract	Accepts students citywide through random lottery.	Renaissance 2010 School
Stopped taking freshmen in fall 2006 and closed at the end of 2008-09; two new schools opened up in fall 2007.	Collins HS	Collins Academy	9-12	9 (9-12)	Performance	Accepts students citywide through random lottery.	AUSL Professional Development School. Renaissance 2010 School. IDS intervention starting in fall 2007.
		North Lawndale College Prep Charter—Collins	9-12	9 (9-12)	Charter	Accepts students citywide through random lottery.	Renaissance 2010 School

TABLE A.1 CONTINUED

Timing of Intervention	Original School Name	New School Name	Grades Served Prior to Intervention	Grades Served First Year after Intervention (at full capacity)	School Governance after Intervention	Attendance Rules	Later Changes and Other Supports
School Turnaround Specialist Program (STSP) Model							
Fall of 2006	Ames MS	—	7–8	7–8	Traditional		
Fall of 2006	Earle ES	—	K–8	K–8	Traditional		
Fall of 2006	Medill ES	—	K–7	K–8	Traditional		Consolidated with Smyth in fall 2009.
Fall of 2006	Jackson ES	—	K–8	K–8	Traditional		
Academy for Urban School Leadership (AUSL) Model							
Fall of 2006	Sherman ES	Sherman School of Excellence	K–8	K–8	Performance	Open to students living in attendance area.	Renaissance 2010 School
Fall of 2007	Harvard ES	Harvard School of Excellence	K–8	K–8	Performance	Open to students living in attendance area.	Renaissance 2010 School
Fall of 2008	Howe ES	Howe Elementary School of Excellence	K–8	K–8	Performance	Open to students living in attendance area. If space is available, applicants living outside the attendance area may attend.	Renaissance 2010 School
Fall of 2008	Orr HS	Orr Academy	9–12	9–12	Performance	Open to students living in attendance area. The College and Career Academies accept students citywide by application.	IDS intervention starting in fall 2008. Renaissance 2010 School.
Fall of 2008	Morton ES	Morton School of Excellence	K–8	K–8	Performance	Open to students living in attendance area. If space is available, applicants living outside the attendance area may attend.	Renaissance 2010 School
Fall of 2009	Dulles ES	Dulles School of Excellence	K–8	K–8	Performance	Open to students living in attendance area. If space is available, applicants living outside the attendance area may attend.	Renaissance 2010 School
Fall of 2009	Johnson ES	Johnson School of Excellence	K–8	K–8	Performance	Open to students living in attendance area. If space is available, applicants living outside the attendance area may attend.	Renaissance 2010 School
Fall of 2009	Bethune ES	Bethune School of Excellence	K–8	K–8	Performance	Open to students living in attendance area. If space is available, applicants living outside the attendance area may attend.	Renaissance 2010 School
Fall of 2010	Curtis ES	Curtis School of Excellence	K–8	K–8	Performance	Open to students living in attendance area. If space is available, applicants living outside the attendance area may attend.	Renaissance 2010 School
Fall of 2010	Deneen ES	Deneen School of Excellence	K–8	K–8	Performance	Open to students living in attendance area. If space is available, applicants living outside the attendance area may attend.	Renaissance 2010 School
Fall of 2010	Bradwell ES	Bradwell School of Excellence	K–8	K–8	Performance	Open to students living in attendance area. If space is available, applicants living outside the attendance area may attend.	Renaissance 2010 School
Fall of 2010	Phillips HS	Phillips Academy HS	9–12	9–12	Performance	Open to students living in attendance area. If space is available, applicants living outside the attendance area may attend.	Renaissance 2010 School
Office of School Improvement (OSI) Model							
Fall of 2008	Copernicus ES	—	K–8	K–8	Traditional		
Fall of 2008	Fulton ES	—	K–8	K–8	Traditional		
Fall of 2008	Harper HS	—	9–12	9–12	Traditional		IDS intervention starting in fall 2008.
Fall of 2009	Fenger HS	—	9–12	9–12	Traditional		
Fall of 2010	Marshall HS	—	9–12	9–12	Traditional		

Notes: Reengineering was a process of peer review of teachers. Teachers with weak skills were supposed to get support from a mentoring teacher for a year and, if no improvement was made, they were counseled out of the profession. Twelve high schools were placed in this category, but few Peer Review Committees were elected and no teachers were reviewed.

Intervention was designed after the delays in the "reengineering" process. Intervention meant that expert teachers in each core subject were installed in the high schools to provide expert assistance to teachers in their department and evaluate the capacity of teachers in their subject area. Teachers who were judged weak were supposed to be fired. Intervention was judged as ineffective by central office staff and eliminated after the 2001–02 school year. Five high schools went through intervention.

Instructional Development System (IDS) focuses on improving the rigor and relevance of high school courses by using a unified system of curricular strategies, classroom materials, assessments, professional development, and personalized teacher coaching. Schools that participate in IDS can choose from two or three instruction options in English, math and science.

Appendix A

TABLE A.2

Schools closed for low academic performance, not included in study

Year	Original School Name	New School Name	Grades Served Prior Change	First Year in Operation	Grades Served by New School First Year (at full capacity)	Type of School
Closed at the End of 2001-02	Williams ES*	Big Picture HS	K-8	Fall 2003	9 (9-12)	Small School
Closed at the End of 2001-02	Terrell ES	Ace Technical	K-8	Fall 2004	9 (9-12)	Charter School
Closed at the End of 2004-05	Grant ES	Marine Military Academy	K-8	Fall 2007	9 (9-12)	Charter School
Closed at the End of 2005-06	Farren ES	The building now houses Attucks Academy	K-8			

Note: *While Williams ES is included in the study and is compared to three elementary schools that were opened in the building after its closure, Big Picture HS is not included as it does not serve any overlapping grades.

Appendix B
Data and Data Sources

This appendix contains information on the data sources and variables used for the analyses in this report. **Table B.1** shows the data sources and which variables came from each one of them. Each of the variables is defined in detail in this appendix grouped by type of analysis.

Definitions of Variables Used in Descriptive Analyses

Student Data

Student data came from Chicago Public Schools 1996/97–2009/10 administrative data, test data, and transcript data.[53] Student addresses were linked to data from the 2000 U.S. Census Bureau at the block group level. The concentration of poverty in a student's neighborhood and social capital were calculated using 2000 U.S. Census Bureau figures. Student variables were defined as follows:

- **Student Identifier.** Student's unique identification code.

- **School Enrollment.** School student attended.

- **Race/Ethnicity.** Whether a student was Asian American, African American, Latino, white, or other.

- **Gender.** Whether a student was male or female.

- **Grade.** Student's grade.

- **Distance Traveled to School.** The distance in miles from the student's address to the school's address was calculated after both addresses were geocoded.

- **Special Education.** Whether a student was receiving special education services.

TABLE B.1

Source of student, teacher, and school variables included in the analysis of intervention and comparison schools in Chicago Public Schools

Variable	Data Source
Students	
Student Identifier	Chicago Public Schools Student Administrative Records
School Enrollment	
Race/Ethnicity	
Gender	
Grade Address	
Special Education	
Birth Date	
Limited English Proficient	
Neighborhood Concentration of Poverty and Social Status	U.S. Census Bureau
Iowa Tests of Basic Skills (ITBS) Scores	Chicago Public Schools Test Data
Illinois Standards Achievement Test (Isat) Scores	
Tests Of Achievement and Proficiency (TAP) scores	
Prairie State Achievement Examination (PSAE) Scores	
Student Absences	Chicago Public Schools Transcript Data
Student Course Performance	
Student Attendance Rate	Illinois State Report Card
Student Truancy Rate	
Student Mobility Rate	
Student Dropout Rate	
Percentage of Students with Limited English Proficiency	
Percentage of Asian American Students	
Percentage of African American Students	
Percentage of Latino Students	
Percentage of white Students	
Percentage of Special Education Students	
Percentage of Students from Low-Income Households	
Teachers	
TeacherIdentifier	Chicago Public Schools Teacher Personnel Records
Active Status	
Gender	
Race/Ethnicity	
Degree attained	
Certification	
First Hired by Chicago Public Schools	
Birth Date	
Schools	
School Size	Illinois State Report Card
School Probation Status Indicator	Chicago Public Schools School-Level Data
School Address	

- **Old for Grade.** A dummy variable to indicate whether a student was older than would be expected for her grade based on school system guidelines and the student's birth date.

- **Neighborhood Concentration of Poverty.** Based on data from the 2000 U.S. Census on the census block group in which students lived. Students' home addresses were used to link each student to a particular block group within the city, which could then be linked to census data on the economic conditions of the student's neighborhood. Two reverse-coded indicators were used to construct these variables, the log of the percentage of household above the poverty line and the log of the percentage of men employed in the block group.

- **Neighborhood Social Status.** Based on data from the 2000 U.S. Census on the census block group in which students lived. Students' home addresses were used to link each student to a particular block group within the city, which could then be linked to census data on the economic conditions of the student's neighborhood. Two indicators were used to construct these variables, the average level of education among adults over age 21 and the log of the percentage of men in the block group employed as managers or executives.

- **Incoming Reading Performance.** For elementary schools, this was the students' prior Iowa Tests of Basic Skills (ITBS) or Illinois Standards Achievement Test (ISAT) reading score. For high schools, this variable was the student's eighth grade test score. To make scores comparable across years, scores from either the ISAT or ITBS were converted into standard deviations from the system mean in each year and for each grade.

Teacher Data

Teacher data were obtained from Chicago Public Schools personnel records for 1996/97–2009/10. Information was not available on teachers in charter and some contract schools because teachers in these schools are employed by independent nonprofit organizations, not by Chicago Public Schools. Teacher variables used in the descriptive analysis include the following:

- **Teacher Identifier.** Teacher's unique identification code.

- **Active Status.** Teachers working in the school at any time between November 1 and June 1 of the academic year.

- **Gender.** Whether a teacher is male or female.

- **Race.** Whether a teacher was Asian American, African American, Latino, white, or other.

- **Advanced Degrees.** Whether a teacher has a master's or doctoral degree. Master's and doctoral degree dummy variables were collapsed to indicate teachers with an advanced degree.

- **Provisional Certification.** Teachers who have not acquired any of the four certificates required in Illinois (elementary education, early childhood education, secondary education, and special education) are assumed to have provisional certification.

- **Years Of Chicago Public Schools Service.** Derived from the date hired into Chicago Public Schools subtracted from November 1 of the academic year.

- **Age.** Calculated using a date of birth variable, where date of birth was subtracted from the November 1 of the intervention year. After 2007, age was calculated using a birth year variable, where the birth year was subtracted from the fall year of intervention.

Definitions of Variables Used for the Propensity Score Calculation

School Data

School data were obtained from Chicago Public Schools 1996/97–2009/10 records and from the Illinois State Report Card. School-level variables include the following:

- **Math Scores.** Mean math score (scores were standardized at the student level by year and grade to have a mean of zero and a standard deviation of one) for the school on either the ITBS or ISAT one year before intervention, two years before intervention, and three years before intervention. Used only for elementary schools.

- **Reading Scores.** Mean reading score (scores were standardized at the student level by year and grade to have a mean of zero and a standard deviation of one) for the school on either the ITBS or ISAT one year before intervention, two years before intervention, and three years before intervention. Used only for elementary schools.

- **Absences.** Average absence rates (absences were standardized at the student level by year and grade to have a mean of zero and a standard deviation of one) for the school one year before intervention, two years before intervention, and three years before intervention. Used only for high schools.

- **On-Track to Graduate Rates.** Average on-track to graduate rates for the school one year before intervention, two years before intervention, and three years before intervention. Used only for high schools.

- **Average Grade 11 Achievement.** Students' composite scores on either the Tests of Achievement and Proficiency (TAP) or the Prairie State Achievement Examination (PSAE) were converted into standard deviations from the system mean in each year. Used only for high schools.

- **Attendance Rate.** Aggregate days of student attendance, divided by the sum of the aggregate days of student attendance and aggregate days of student absence, multiplied by 100. Used only for elementary schools.

- **Truancy Rate.** Number of chronic truants, divided by the average daily enrollment, multiplied by 100. Chronic truants include students subject to compulsory attendance who have been absent without valid cause for 10 percent or more of the previous 180 regular attendance days.

- **Mobility Rate.** It is the sum of the number of students who transferred out and the number of students who transferred in, divided by the average daily enrollment, multiplied by 100. Students are counted each time they transfer out or in during the reporting year, which includes from the first school day in October to the last day of the school year.

- **Dropout Rates.** The percentage of students dropping out in a given school year. The dropout rate is based on the number of students in grades 9-12 who drop out in a given year and is calculated according to the Illinois State Board of Education formula, which includes all students enrolled in Chicago Public Schools as of the end of September in a given school year. Used only for high schools.

- **Percentage of Limited English Proficient Students.** The count of limited English proficient students divided by the total fall enrollment, multiplied by 100. Limited English proficient students are students who are eligible for bilingual education.

- **Percentage of Asian American Students.** The percentage of Asian American students in a school.

- **Percentage of African American Students.** The percentage of African American students in a school.

- **Percentage of Latino Students.** The percentage of Latino students in a school.

- **Percentage of white Students.** The percentage of white students in a school.

- **Percentage of Special Education Students.** The count of students who are eligible to receive special education services and therefore have an individualized education program, divided by the total fall enrollment, multiplied by 100.

- **Percentage of Students from Low-Income Households.** Students ages 3-17 in households receiving public aid, in institutions for neglected or delinquent children, supported in foster homes with public funds, or eligible to receive free or reduced-price lunches. The percentage of low-income students is the count of low-income students, divided by the total fall enrollment, multiplied by 100.

- **School Size.** Total student enrollment in a school in the fall of the school year.

- **Enrollment in Grade 9.** Total student enrollment in grade 9 of the school in the fall of the school year.

- **Probation Status.** Whether a school was on probation the year before intervention, two years before intervention, or three years before intervention.

Definitions of Outcome Variables Used for the Multilevel Models

For Elementary Schools

Two outcome variables were used for elementary schools:

- **Reading Score.** ISAT scores were used for students in grades 3-8 over 2005/06–2009/10. ITBS scores were used for students in grades 3-8 over 1996/97–2004/05. Z-scores were used to standardize scores from both exams for comparison. The Z-score is the number of standard deviations that the score is from the mean of the distribution.

- **Math Score.** ISAT scores were used for students in grades 3-8 over 2005/06–2009/10. ITBS scores were used for students in grades 3-8 over 1996/97–2004/05. Z-scores were used to standardize exam scores from both exams for comparison. The Z-score is the number of standard deviations that the score is from the mean of the distribution.

For High Schools

Two outcome variables were used for high schools:

- **Absences.** Before 2007-08, absences were calculated using a measure of the average days absent, totaling all course absences and dividing by the number of courses. This measure takes into account not only full-day absences but also course-cutting behavior. In 2008, the Chicago Public Schools district changed its data collection and measurement system and now reports only full days absent by semester. To standardize data and compare them across years, Z-scores were calculated by standardizing the days absent by grade and year to have a mean of zero and standard deviation of one. Only fall absences were considered because spring absences during the first year in which the new data system was used were unavailable.

- **On-Track to Graduate Rates.** Indicator for whether a student is on-track to graduate by the end of ninth grade. Students at the end of ninth grade who have accumulated enough credits to move on to tenth grade and have no more than one semester F are on-track to graduate. These students are three and a half times more likely to graduate than students who are off-track.

Independent Variables for Both Elementary and High Schools

- **Race.** Whether a student was Asian American, African American, Latino, white, or other.

- **Gender.** Whether a student is male or female.

- **Grade.** Student's grade level.

- **Prior Achievement.** For elementary schools, this was a student's prior ITBS or ISAT score. For high schools, this was the student's eighth grade composite reading score. Students in Chicago Public Schools took either the ISAT or ITBS test in eighth grade before entering high school. To make scores comparable across years, reading and math scores from either the ISAT or ITBS were converted into standard deviations from the system mean in each year and for each grade.

- **Special Education.** Whether a student is receiving special education services. Students receiving special education services are students who are eligible to receive special education services and have an individualized education program.

- **Old for Grade.** Whether a student was old for grade was indicated by a dummy variable to indicate whether a student was older than would be expected from school system guidelines given the grade the student was attending.

- **Limited English Proficiency.** Whether a student is eligible for bilingual education (only in elementary schools analyses).

- **Neighborhood Concentration of Poverty.** Based on data from the 2000 U.S. Census on the census block group in which students lived. Students' home addresses were used to link each student to a particular block group within the city, which could then be linked to census data on the economic conditions of the student's neighborhood. Two indicators were used to construct these variables: the log of the percentage of families above the poverty line and the log of the percentage of men employed in the block group.

- **Neighborhood Social Status.** Based on data from the 2000 U.S. Census on the census block group in which students lived. Students' home addresses were used to link each student to a particular block group within the city, which could then be linked to census data on the economic conditions of the student's neighborhood. Two indicators were used to construct these variables: the average level of education among adults over age 21 and the log of the percentage of men in the block group employed as managers or executives.

Appendix C
Research Methods and Results

Analyses of the Characteristics of Students and Teachers

In order to examine changes in the composition of students in intervention schools, we examined the characteristics of students who attended schools in September of the year before the intervention took place and in September of the first year of the intervention. The sample of students consisted of those students who were in the schools at these time points. Data on student body composition come from individual student administrative records that CCSR receives from CPS, including student race, age, gender, academic achievement, and special education status (**see Appendix B** for a description of the data and data sources). We use students' home addresses to determine whether schools continue to serve students from the same neighborhoods, and we link addresses to information from the census at the block-group level to create indicators of poverty and social status in students' census block group to determine whether the types of students being served by the school changed after intervention.

Our analyses only compare students in similar grades. (**See Appendix A** for a list of the grade levels served by the old and new schools.) For example, School A may have been a 9-12 high school prior to closure, but served only ninth grade upon reopening and added an additional grade each year. In that case, our analysis includes a comparison of the new ninth grade students with the last group of ninth grade students to have gone through that school before intervention. **Table C.1** provides the descriptive student characteristics by school, as well as the number of students in the sample. The last column shows the percent of students who came back to these schools in the first year of intervention and the comparable period before that. **Table C.2** shows the rate of reenrollment from September to September in two consecutive years after the intervention was in place.

In order to examine changes in the composition of teachers in intervention schools, we examined teachers who worked at these schools in the academic year before the intervention took place and the first academic year of the intervention. We used personnel records from CPS (**see Appendix B** for details on data sources and variables). These records contain information on degrees (bachelor's, master's, or doctorate); experience within CPS; demographic characteristics (e.g., age, race, gender); and certifications. CPS personnel records do not include information on teachers in charter schools or contract schools; therefore, these schools were not included in this analysis. This is the case for three schools in the Closure and Restart model because those three reopened as charter or contract schools. We do not have data on teachers for the schools that most recently underwent intervention. In particular five schools, four under AUSl and one under OSI are not included in the teacher analyses. **Table C.3** provides descriptive teacher characteristics by school and the sample size of each comparison.

TABLE C.1
Descriptive student characteristics before and after intervention, by school

School Name	Timing	Percent Male	Percent African American	Percent Latino	Percent Old for Grade	Percent Special Education	Average Neighborhood Concentration of Poverty (measured in standard deviations)	Average Neighborhood Social Status (measured in standard deviations)	Average Distance Traveled to School (miles)	Average Incoming Reading Performance (measured in standard deviations)	Total Number of Students Enrolled	Percent Students Reenrolled (of those eligible)[A]
Reconstitution Model												
DuSable HS	Fall 1996	46.8%	99.5%	0.1%	57.7%	17.2%	1.43	-0.73	Data Not Available	-0.46	1,481	58.7%
	Fall 1997	50.2%	99.5%	0.3%	48.8%	21.3%	1.44	-0.70	1.08	-0.46	1,183	55.8%
Robeson HS	Fall 1996	54.6%	99.9%	0.1%	58.1%	17.2%	0.66	-0.36	Data Not Available	-0.40	1,371	67.0%
	Fall 1997	55.8%	99.4%	0.3%	58.9%	20.8%	0.68	-0.35	1.29	-0.38	1,179	62.3%
Harper HS	Fall 1996	54.0%	99.3%	0.6%	53.2%	17.0%	0.49	-0.51	Data Not Available	-0.50	1,631	62.9%
	Fall 1997	55.0%	99.0%	0.8%	49.1%	18.2%	0.49	-0.53	0.98	-0.53	1,476	59.5%
Phillips HS	Fall 1996	53.4%	99.9%	0.0%	57.3%	21.4%	1.49	-0.57	Data Not Available	-0.61	1,194	50.9%
	Fall 1997	49.1%	99.6%	0.1%	57.8%	22.3%	1.43	-0.56	1.40	-0.61	982	61.6%
Englewood HS	Fall 1996	53.1%	99.4%	0.2%	56.4%	18.7%	0.87	-0.56	Data Not Available	-0.52	1,366	66.5%
	Fall 1997	50.0%	99.9%	0.0%	50.2%	20.0%	0.86	-0.50	1.40	-0.45	1,061	58.4%
King HS	Fall 1996	47.8%	99.3%	0.4%	46.2%	15.1%	1.26	-0.61	Data Not Available	-0.43	827	59.7%
	Fall 1997	45.5%	99.4%	0.4%	40.8%	15.9%	1.22	-0.55	1.71	-0.42	679	60.9%
Orr HS	Fall 1996	49.8%	94.4%	5.2%	53.0%	12.8%	0.51	-0.70	Data Not Available	-0.50	1,306	61.7%
	Fall 1997	52.1%	92.5%	7.4%	57.4%	15.1%	0.52	-0.72	1.01	-0.45	1,060	56.8%
Closure and Restart Model												
Dodge ES	Fall 2001	49.0%	99.7%	0.3%	29.5%	23.7%	0.93	-0.54	0.93	-0.54	312	57.1%
	Fall 2003	50.1%	99.4%	0.3%	31.2%	13.6%	0.98	-0.52	1.18	-0.38	359	46.5%
Williams ES	Fall 2001	47.5%	99.7%	0.0%	21.6%	7.7%	1.77	-0.72	0.31	-0.43	727	68.9%
	Fall 2003	53.3%	99.7%	0.0%	28.7%	6.0%	1.61	-0.65	1.36	-0.50	383	31.1%
Howland ES	Fall 2004	48.7%	97.4%	2.6%	50.0%	10.5%	1.83	-0.57	0.24	-0.38	76	38.7%
	Fall 2006	56.3%	99.2%	0.8%	17.6%	5.9%	1.12	-0.58	1.49	-0.30	119	15.5%
Bunche ES	Fall 2004	52.2%	99.3%	0.0%	24.1%	5.5%	1.16	-0.67	0.42	-0.46	274	41.6%
	Fall 2006	46.5%	100.0%	0.0%	7.4%	3.5%	0.90	-0.40	1.63	0.09	202	11.8%
Englewood HS	Fall 2004	59.1%	99.5%	0.3%	48.3%	27.8%	1.09	-0.41	1.58	-0.60	381	28.6%
	Fall 2006[B]	99.4%	99.4%	0.6%	33.3%	14.4%	0.91	-0.32	2.23	-0.17	174	0.0%
Morse ES	Fall 2005	51.0%	98.7%	1.3%	13.7%	8.5%	0.98	-0.73	0.46	-0.26	153	41.8%
	Fall 2007	44.0%	86.2%	12.9%	2.6%	5.2%	0.76	-0.49	1.82	-0.21	116	11.4%
Frazier ES	Fall 2005	46.5%	99.3%	0.7%	31.1%	9.0%	1.21	-0.75	0.72	-0.35	299	60.2%
	Fall 2007	47.8%	97.8%	1.1%	11.0%	7.4%	1.04	-0.59	1.77	-0.40	272	8.9%
Collins HS	Fall 2005	53.1%	99.4%	0.6%	51.8%	26.4%	1.25	-0.60	1.51	-0.46	326	46.7%
	Fall 2007	40.7%	95.8%	4.2%	26.2%	19.2%	1.03	-0.59	1.86	-0.23	214	0.0%
School Turnaround Specialist Program Model												
Ames MS	Fall 2005	50.7%	7.3%	90.4%	28.6%	16.4%	0.28	-1.09	0.48	-0.27	768	76.9%
	Fall 2006	46.8%	7.4%	90.5%	28.3%	15.1%	0.27	-1.08	0.58	-0.22	819	88.6%
Earle ES	Fall 2005	50.9%	99.8%	0.0%	27.0%	12.0%	1.35	-0.84	0.43	-0.39	548	69.8%
	Fall 2006	51.5%	100.0%	0.0%	26.5%	9.8%	1.34	-0.80	0.52	-0.59	480	64.1%
Medill ES	Fall 2005	49.8%	99.5%	0.5%	32.9%	13.2%	1.82	-1.28	0.51	-0.61	219	68.6%
	Fall 2006	49.7%	100.0%	0.0%	30.1%	15.0%	1.81	-1.25	0.33	-0.85	173	72.1%
Jackson ES	Fall 2005	61.7%	98.9%	1.1%	32.9%	29.3%	0.39	0.07	0.95	-0.45	368	74.7%
	Fall 2006	62.3%	99.2%	0.8%	34.4%	27.0%	0.39	0.07	0.82	-0.54	355	75.2%

Appendix C

TABLE C.1: CONTINUED

Descriptive student characteristics before and after intervention, by school

School Name	Timing	Percent Male	Percent African American	Percent Latino	Percent Old for Grade	Percent Special Education	Average Neighborhood Concentration of Poverty (measured in standard deviations)	Average Neighborhood Social Status (measured in standard deviations)	Average Distance Traveled to School (miles)	Average Incoming Reading Performance (measured in standard deviations)	Total Number of Students Enrolled	Percent Students Reenrolled (of those eligible)[A]
Academy for Urban School Leadership Model												
Sherman ES	Fall 2005	51.2%	98.6%	1.3%	27.4%	9.3%	1.08	-0.54	0.36	-0.46	559	73.3%
	Fall 2006	51.3%	97.8%	1.7%	25.9%	11.9%	1.10	-0.51	0.36	-0.64	587	72.7%
Harvard ES	Fall 2006	54.0%	99.0%	0.4%	30.4%	6.5%	1.04	-0.30	0.45	-0.69	494	65.8%
	Fall 2007	54.9%	98.8%	0.8%	23.7%	5.9%	1.09	-0.27	0.38	-0.58	490	68.1%
Howe ES	Fall 2007	49.0%	99.6%	0.2%	23.6%	11.3%	0.81	-0.55	0.32	-0.63	559	66.0%
	Fall 2008	49.1%	99.6%	0.2%	18.3%	10.2%	0.79	-0.55	0.43	-0.41	491	68.9%
Orr HS	Fall 2007	50.8%	90.6%	8.8%	46.4%	29.9%	0.76	-0.65	1.29	-0.53	1,379	67.7%
	Fall 2008	51.8%	91.3%	8.5%	39.6%	29.0%	0.79	-0.64	1.25	-0.53	1,190	65.2%
Morton ES	Fall 2007	48.2%	98.0%	2.0%	32.2%	12.5%	1.01	-0.86	0.57	-0.74	255	52.1%
	Fall 2008	50.8%	95.0%	4.6%	28.2%	14.3%	0.97	-0.84	0.60	-0.55	238	57.1%
Dulles ES	Fall 2008	47.1%	99.7%	0.0%	19.7%	8.9%	1.42	-0.84	0.27	-0.55	395	64.0%
	Fall 2009	49.0%	99.8%	0.0%	18.3%	7.3%	1.41	-0.82	0.26	-0.40	410	76.6%
Johnson ES	Fall 2008	49.4%	99.1%	0.9%	20.4%	14.0%	1.61	-0.65	0.47	-0.44	235	61.6%
	Fall 2009	46.7%	100.0%	0.0%	18.6%	11.6%	1.57	-0.68	0.74	-0.43	242	63.1%
Bethune ES	Fall 2008	51.3%	99.4%	0.6%	31.8%	8.5%	1.17	-0.48	0.43	-0.67	318	76.0%
	Fall 2009	52.8%	100.0%	0.0%	30.2%	10.3%	1.19	-0.46	0.41	-0.72	341	70.9%
Curtis ES	Fall 2009	48.6%	98.3%	1.2%	22.6%	9.0%	0.96	-0.50	0.52	-0.45	424	72.4%
	Fall 2010	49.9%	99.5%	0.5%	23.5%	9.1%	0.95	-0.51	0.54	-0.47	417	70.0%
Deneen ES	Fall 2009	49.9%	99.1%	0.4%	22.4%	11.1%	0.43	-0.03	0.69	-0.39	445	70.3%
	Fall 2010	52.4%	97.7%	0.7%	19.1%	12.3%	0.51	-0.11	0.93	-0.34	439	69.4%
Bradwell ES	Fall 2009	53.5%	99.7%	0.3%	30.2%	9.5%	0.70	-0.26	0.47	-0.48	609	52.9%
	Fall 2010	51.9%	98.9%	0.8%	26.1%	10.3%	0.65	-0.23	0.51	-0.43	663	65.1%
Phillips HS	Fall 2009	50.7%	98.4%	0.4%	48.3%	22.3%	0.75	-0.16	1.90	-0.44	744	65.2%
	Fall 2010	50.4%	97.0%	1.9%	45.7%	21.5%	0.73	-0.10	2.14	-0.41	685	69.1%
Office of School Improvement Model												
Copernicus ES	Fall 2007	49.9%	98.9%	0.3%	27.5%	11.6%	1.13	-0.41	0.47	-0.79	353	65.5%
	Fall 2008	54.0%	99.4%	0.0%	24.9%	10.5%	1.17	-0.44	0.57	-0.57	313	63.5%
Fulton ES	Fall 2007	53.4%	84.9%	14.8%	27.9%	6.8%	1.00	-0.39	0.49	-0.68	577	54.2%
	Fall 2008	54.7%	84.1%	15.4%	23.4%	7.8%	0.99	-0.38	0.53	-0.63	591	64.6%
Harper HS	Fall 2007	57.7%	99.5%	0.2%	62.1%	26.8%	1.03	-0.54	0.93	-0.58	1,274	70.2%
	Fall 2008	52.4%	99.7%	0.1%	56.8%	25.6%	1.03	-0.53	0.97	-0.53	946	55.3%
Fenger HS	Fall 2008	50.0%	99.4%	0.2%	38.4%	21.3%	0.62	-0.24	1.51	-0.51	1,212	71.2%
	Fall 2009	48.5%	99.4%	0.3%	40.0%	19.0%	0.67	-0.25	1.44	-0.52	1,187	73.8%
Marshall HS	Fall 2009	56.3%	99.5%	0.4%	43.1%	25.1%	1.08	-0.41	1.73	-0.44	996	64.1%
	Fall 2010	56.8%	99.1%	0.8%	67.2%	24.8%	1.05	-0.40	1.90	-0.43	775	65.7%

Notes: A Percentage of students reenrolled was calculated between years reflecting length of closure for Closure and Restart schools. For example, if a school closed in fall 2001 and reopened in 2003, the percentage of students reenrolled in fall 2003 is calculated using student enrollment in fall 2001 and fall 2003, and the percentage of students reenrolled in fall 2001 is calculated using student enrollment from fall 1999 to fall 2001 to reflect the two-year gap. To make these numbers analogous, the same grades are compared both times.

B Two high schools opened in this building, but in two different years: one in fall 2006 and the other in fall 2007. Student body characteristics are based on the enrollment of the school that opened up in fall 2006 in that building.

TABLE C.2

Percent of students reenrolling in the years after intervention (of those eligible), by school

Reenrollment from Fall to Fall in Two Consecutive Years after Intervention

School Name	Year 1 of Intervention From Fall Year Prior to Fall Year 1	Year 2 of Intervention From Fall Year 1 to Fall Year 2	Year 3 of Intervention From Fall Year 2 to Fall Year 3	Year 4 of Intervention From Fall Year 3 to Fall Year 4
Reconstitution Model				
DuSable HS	55.8%	67.2%	65.3%	65.3%
Robeson HS	62.3%	56.7%	64.5%	64.9%
Harper HS	59.5%	59.3%	62.2%	67.7%
Phillips HS	61.6%	55.3%	67.4%	64.2%
Englewood HS	58.4%	63.7%	64.9%	67.2%
King HS	60.9%	64.7%	67.4%	69.3%
Orr HS	56.8%	65.5%	60.7%	66.8%
Closure and Restart Model				
Dodge ES	Data Not Available	70.9%	79.4%	83.8%
Williams ES	Data Not Available	69.3%	68.2%	62.8%
Howland ES	Data Not Available	42.0%	77.0%	76.4%
Bunche ES	Data Not Available	83.6%	80.4%	75.7%
Englewood HS	Data Not Available	68.9%	81.8%	81.5%
Morse ES	Data Not Available	83.6%	82.6%	78.2%
Frazier ES	Data Not Available	72.7%	81.1%	77.2%
Collins HS	Data Not Available	87.9%	82.1%	80.5%
School Turnaround Specialist Program Model				
Ames MS	88.6%	84.4%	86.2%	89.1%
Earle ES	64.1%	60.4%	68.8%	59.2%
Medill ES	72.7%	82.0%	Data Not Available	Data Not Available
Jackson ES	75.2%	66.6%	73.0%	75.9%
Academy for Urban School Leadership Model				
Sherman ES	72.7%	77.1%	66.0%	64.1%
Harvard ES	68.1%	70.7%	70.7%	73.1%
Howe ES	68.9%	80.2%	81.8%	80.3%
Orr HS	65.2%	68.9%	62.3%	62.0%
Morton ES	57.1%	65.3%	72.3%	75.7%
Dulles ES	76.6%	82.8%	80.4%	Data Not Available
Johnson ES	63.1%	78.8%	70.5%	Data Not Available
Bethune ES	70.9%	70.3%	74.4%	Data Not Available
Curtis ES	70.0%	Data Not Available	Data Not Available	Data Not Available
Deneen ES	69.4%	Data Not Available	Data Not Available	Data Not Available
Bradwell ES	65.1%	Data Not Available	Data Not Available	Data Not Available
Phillips HS	69.1%	Data Not Available	Data Not Available	Data Not Available
Office of School Improvement Model				
Copernicus ES	63.5%	69.7%	74.1%	Data Not Available
Fulton ES	64.6%	64.2%	70.6%	Data Not Available
Harper HS	55.3%	66.6%	73.8%	Data Not Available
Fenger HS	73.8%	73.2%	73.2%	Data Not Available
Marshall HS	65.7%	Data Not Available	Data Not Available	Data Not Available

TABLE C.3

Descriptive teacher characteristics before and after intervention, by school

School Name	Timing	N	Percent Male	Percent White	Percent African American	Percent Asian American	Percent Latino	Percent Advanced Degrees	Average Age	Average Years of CPS Service	Percent Provisional Certification
Reconstitution Model											
DuSable HS	Fall 1996	86	44.2%	32.6%	65.1%	1.2%	1.2%	57.0%	49.38	16.87	10.5%
	Fall 1997	60	46.7%	36.7%	61.7%	1.7%	0.0%	60.0%	48.56	16.29	10.0%
Robeson HS	Fall 1996	78	33.3%	24.4%	75.6%	0.0%	0.0%	59.0%	50.67	19.85	3.8%
	Fall 1997	62	29.0%	29.0%	67.7%	3.2%	0.0%	50.0%	47.29	15.48	11.3%
Harper HS	Fall 1996	87	39.1%	33.3%	64.4%	2.3%	0.0%	54.0%	45.34	14.92	3.4%
	Fall 1997	80	37.5%	28.8%	71.3%	0.0%	0.0%	52.5%	44.30	13.15	7.5%
Phillips HS	Fall 1996	91	40.7%	29.7%	69.2%	1.1%	0.0%	53.8%	48.98	14.20	11.0%
	Fall 1997	60	41.7%	26.7%	68.3%	3.3%	1.7%	51.7%	45.38	10.82	10.0%
Englewood HS	Fall 1996	80	46.3%	28.8%	71.3%	0.0%	0.0%	48.8%	50.52	17.29	3.8%
	Fall 1997	64	35.9%	17.2%	82.8%	0.0%	0.0%	53.1%	47.66	16.82	15.6%
King HS	Fall 1996	57	31.6%	19.3%	80.7%	0.0%	0.0%	61.4%	52.15	19.58	0.0%
	Fall 1997	39	17.9%	20.5%	79.5%	0.0%	0.0%	56.4%	49.07	18.04	5.1%
Orr HS	Fall 1996	91	40.7%	48.4%	49.5%	1.1%	1.1%	49.5%	50.21	18.25	4.4%
	Fall 1997	73	35.6%	41.1%	56.2%	1.4%	1.4%	49.3%	47.07	15.84	9.6%
Closure and Restart Model											
Dodge ES	Fall 2001	22	27.3%	36.4%	63.6%	0.0%	0.0%	63.6%	46.80	13.12	9.1%
	Fall 2003	26	11.5%	46.2%	53.8%	0.0%	0.0%	88.5%	41.90	11.21	0.0%
Williams ES	Fall 2001	43	16.3%	25.6%	72.1%	0.0%	2.3%	51.2%	49.16	15.94	4.7%
	Fall 2003	30	6.7%	40.0%	46.7%	10.0%	3.3%	40.0%	36.49	6.71	0.0%
Howland ES	Fall 2004	22	13.6%	54.5%	41.0%	4.5%	0.0%	27.3%	39.86	8.69	4.6%
	Fall 2006						Data Not Available				
Bunche ES	Fall 2004	16	18.8%	25.0%	75.0%	0.0%	0.0%	68.8%	51.79	20.11	3.3%
	Fall 2006						Data Not Available				
Englewood HS[A,B]	Fall 2006	37	37.8%	27.0%	62.2%	2.7%	5.4%	0.0%	47.62	13.15	2.7%
	Fall 2007	12	41.7%	83.3%	16.7%	0.0%	0.0%	0.0%	30.27	2.51	33.3%
Morse ES	Fall 2005	30	13.0%	43.3%	50.0%	3.3%	0.0%	46.7%	43.21	9.99	3.3%
	Fall 2007						Data Not Available				
Frazier ES[A]	Fall 2005	25	16.0%	28.0%	64.0%	8.0%	0.0%	0.0%	53.16	16.94	0.0%
	Fall 2007	9	11.1%	66.7%	33.3%	0.0%	0.0%	0.0%	53.97	10.50	0.0%
Collins HS[A,B]	Fall 2006	43	44.2%	34.9%	62.8%	2.3%	0.0%	0.0%	54.81	16.51	4.7%
	Fall 2007	8	75.0%	62.5%	37.5%	0.0%	0.0%	0.0%	39.13	3.07	25.0%
School Turnaround Specialist Program Model											
Ames MS	Fall 2005	47	36.2%	53.2%	14.9%	4.3%	25.5%	59.6%	42.90	8.83	4.3%
	Fall 2006	43	46.5%	41.9%	18.6%	2.3%	34.9%	58.1%	43.11	9.39	9.3%
Earle ES	Fall 2005	24	12.5%	16.7%	83.3%	0.0%	0.0%	70.8%	48.90	17.17	0.0%
	Fall 2006	28	21.4%	14.3%	85.7%	0.0%	0.0%	50.0%	47.78	11.09	14.3%
Medill ES	Fall 2005	16	0.0%	56.3%	25.0%	6.3%	12.5%	12.5%	44.65	13.12	0.0%
	Fall 2006	14	7.1%	35.7%	50.0%	14.3%	0.0%	28.6%	44.64	7.87	14.3%
Jackson ES	Fall 2005	29	13.8%	20.7%	79.3%	0.0%	0.0%	58.6%	45.75	15.19	0.0%
	Fall 2006	31	9.7%	16.1%	83.9%	0.0%	0.0%	54.8%	46.09	15.18	9.7%
Academy for Urban School Leadership Model											
Sherman ES	Fall 2005	31	19.4%	38.7%	54.8%	6.5%	0.0%	45.2%	44.88	11.30	6.5%
	Fall 2006	31	19.4%	41.9%	51.6%	3.2%	3.2%	64.5%	37.62	5.23	6.5%
Harvard ES	Fall 2006	26	15.4%	26.9%	73.1%	0.0%	0.0%	0.0%	51.64	14.14	7.7%
	Fall 2007	25	24.0%	28.0%	68.0%	0.0%	4.0%	0.0%	40.74	5.48	4.0%
Howe ES	Fall 2007	27	22.2%	18.5%	74.1%	0.0%	7.4%	55.6%	49.38	11.35	14.8%
	Fall 2008	30	20.0%	46.7%	43.3%	0.0%	10.0%	73.3%	33.11	2.67	13.3%
Orr HS	Fall 2007	98	43.9%	61.2%	30.6%	3.1%	3.1%	58.2%	44.86	7.16	17.3%
	Fall 2008	91	36.3%	45.1%	45.1%	2.2%	5.5%	59.3%	44.82	5.37	26.4%
Morton ES	Fall 2007	22	4.5%	31.8%	63.6%	0.0%	4.5%	27.3%	50.81	10.41	13.6%
	Fall 2008	18	27.8%	66.7%	22.2%	5.6%	5.6%	55.6%	41.23	3.36	11.1%
Dulles ES	Fall 2008	27	14.8%	11.1%	88.9%	0.0%	0.0%	48.1%	51.24	14.16	0.0%
	Fall 2009	24	16.7%	70.8%	29.2%	0.0%	0.0%	54.2%	43.37	2.29	12.5%
Johnson ES	Fall 2008	16	25.0%	43.8%	50.0%	0.0%	6.3%	31.3%	50.40	11.23	6.3%
	Fall 2009	17	11.8%	41.2%	58.8%	0.0%	0.0%	70.6%	37.52	3.61	5.9%
Bethune ES	Fall 2008	19	21.1%	31.6%	63.2%	5.3%	0.0%	52.6%	46.75	7.74	5.3%
	Fall 2009	26	15.4%	53.8%	38.5%	3.8%	3.8%	65.4%	40.75	1.56	11.5%
Curtis ES	Fall 2009	22	13.6%	13.6%	86.4%	0.0%	0.0%	68.2%	51.20	18.68	0.0%
	Fall 2010						Data Not Available				
Deneen ES	Fall 2009	28	14.3%	21.4%	75.0%	3.6%	0.0%	64.3%	52.55	12.77	21.4%
	Fall 2010						Data Not Available				
Bradwell ES	Fall 2009	36	13.9%	19.4%	80.6%	0.0%	0.0%	66.7%	54.01	16.33	0.0%
	Fall 2010						Data Not Available				
Phillips HS	Fall 2009	44	34.1%	36.4%	56.8%	6.8%	0.0%	68.2%	58.38	14.76	4.5%
	Fall 2010						Data Not Available				
Office of School Improvement Model											
Copernicus ES	Fall 2007	22	18.2%	27.3%	63.6%	0.0%	4.5%	54.5%	45.28	8.47	13.6%
	Fall 2008	18	11.1%	33.3%	55.6%	11.1%	0.0%	66.7%	42.03	9.20	27.8%
Fulton ES	Fall 2007	37	10.8%	29.7%	56.8%	0.0%	10.8%	27.0%	48.34	9.96	10.8%
	Fall 2008	30	26.7%	53.3%	33.3%	0.0%	13.3%	26.7%	38.73	3.24	26.7%
Harper HS	Fall 2007	80	30.0%	38.8%	60.0%	0.0%	1.3%	65.0%	49.75	12.17	12.5%
	Fall 2008	78	34.6%	43.6%	47.4%	7.7%	1.3%	46.2%	44.10	4.18	26.9%
Fenger HS	Fall 2008	80	37.5%	28.8%	62.5%	3.8%	3.8%	56.3%	49.57	9.34	8.8%
	Fall 2009	87	34.5%	46.0%	46.0%	6.9%	1.1%	42.5%	45.31	3.30	32.2%
Marshall HS	Fall 2009	70	35.7%	28.6%	62.9%	4.3%	4.3%	58.6%	50.92	14.73	5.7%
	Fall 2010						Data Not Available				

Notes: **A** Two schools opened in these buildings, but data was available for only one of the schools. The second school was either a charter or a contract school.
B These two high schools were phased out grade-by-grade; at the same time, new schools opened in the building. Comparisons among teachers were made on the basis of the teacher workforce the first year of the new school, and the teacher workforce left in the phasing-out school the prior year.

Analyses on Student Achievement in Grades 3-8

We examined two outcomes for elementary schools, test scores in reading and test scores in math. Students in CPS took achievement tests each year in grades 3 through 8. For this analysis, students' scores are combined across the grades by including dummy variables for grade level in the statistical models. This produces an average score for the entire school, regardless of which grade levels they serve. Scores were converted into standard deviations from the system mean in each year and for each grade; thus, they can be interpreted as the degree to which students' scores were different from the system average in their grade in that year. A score that is half a standard deviation below the mean is at about the 30th percentile in the district. Standardizing within each year provides an automatic adjustment for any system wide trends that should not be attributed to the intervention, and for differences in tests, or scoring of tests, that may have occurred across the years.

Sample

Schools that underwent one of the five school interventions studied in this project were all low-performing schools on probation in the year the district decided to intervene. The district put schools on probation on the basis of a combination of factors, but all schools at risk of intervention had scores that fell below a certain threshold. The specific policy changed over time, and this is reflected in the number of schools on probation each year. Our two-prong method for identifying comparison schools included only schools that were on probation in the year the treated school was identified for intervention because the district would consider only these schools for the kinds of interventions we studied. In addition, we restricted the pool of potential comparison schools to those that were in existence for at least four years prior to the year the treated school(s) underwent intervention. **Table C.4** shows the number of elementary schools that were on probation during the years schools in the treatment group were identified for intervention, and had at least three years of test scores before that year. The 22 elementary schools that underwent intervention were not included as potential matching schools, even if they were on probation during periods prior to or subsequent to their own reform.

Group-Based Trajectory Analysis

Since schools went through interventions at different points in time, an analysis of test trend growth patterns was done for each time period during which an intervention took place. For example, two schools, Dodge and Williams, learned in the middle of the 2001-02 academic year that they were going to be closed at the end of that academic year. To discern groups of schools with prior trends similar to those of Dodge and Williams, we examined test growth patterns among the 41 schools on probation in the 2001-02 year; trends patterns were based on test scores in the three prior years (from 1998-99 through 2000-01).[54] We ran this analysis separately for reading and math in seven separate time periods, corresponding with the years that schools were identified for intervention. The analyses were performed with SAS using *proc traj*, the latent class procedure developed by Bobby L. Jones. Determining the number of distinct groups of schools from the reading and math trajectories was based on the Bayesian information criterion (BIC) statistic. Solutions to latent class models are prone to errors that arise from the likelihood of local maximum solutions, rather than the global maximum solution. Solutions with many latent classes have a greater likelihood of this error. Even though the number of groups we have uncovered is not large, we addressed this problem by estimating the models several times with different starting points and checking for consistency.

The trajectory information ensured that schools not only were similar in their outcome measure right before the intervention, but also had been on similar trends prior to intervention. Without this information, it is possible that we would have identified comparison schools that were at a similar level right before intervention, but had been on very different trajectories in the years prior; one school might have been improving while another was declining. **Figure C.1** displays the reading and math trajectories estimated by latent class analysis for all schools in each of the seven time periods. To explain, the first graph shows that in the time period 1999-2001, schools on probation could be classified into three groups based on statistically different trajectories on their reading scores. The two schools that underwent intervention a year later were classified into groups 1 and 2. Therefore, comparison schools were chosen from those schools that had the same prior trajectories as the schools that underwent intervention— groups 1 and 2. The percentages displayed in the graphs denote the proportion of all eligible schools in that time period that were classified into the various trajectory groups. In general, the schools that underwent interventions fell into those groups with the lowest reading and math scores. In some cases, the trajectories of schools that received interventions were decreasing over time, but this is not always the case, further supporting our use of the group trajectory analysis to identify comparison schools. **See Table C.4** for a description of eligible schools within each intervention period, the number of patterns observed within each period, which patterns the intervened schools were in, and the number of potential control schools to be used in the final hierarchical analyses.

TABLE C.4
Elementary schools that matched selection criteria to be in the comparison group

Intervention Period	Number of Schools on Probation	Observed Test Trend Patterns in Intervention Schools	Number of Intervention Schools Displaying Pattern	Number of Control Schools Displaying Pattern
Schools Identified 2001-02 (On probation 2001-02 year; trend data: 1998-99 to 2000-01)	41	READING 1; Math 1 READING 2; Math 2 Out of 3 test trend patterns in reading and 3 in math.	1 1	4 16
Schools Identified 2004-05 (On probation 2004-05 year; trend data: 2001-02 to 2003-04)	147	READING 1; Math 1 Out of 4 test trend patterns in reading and 3 in math.	2	7
Schools Identified 2005-06 (On probation 2005-06 year; trend data: 2002-03 to 2004-05)	176	READING 1; Math 1 READING 2; Math 1 READING 2; Math 2 READING 3; Math 4 Out of 5 test trend patterns in reading and 4 in math.	3 1 2 1	15 20 29 4
Schools Identified 2006-07 (On probation 2006-07 year; trend data: 2003-04 to 2005-06)	36	READING 1; Math 1 Out of 2 test trend patterns in reading and 2 in math.	1	18
Schools Identified 2007-08 (On probation 2007-08 year; trend data: 2004-05 to 2006-07)	161	READING 1; Math 1 Out of 5 test trend patterns in reading and 3 in math.	4	31
Schools Identified 2008-09 (On probation 2008-09 year; trend data: 2005-06 to 2007-08)	199	READING 2; Math 2 Out of 4 test trend patterns in reading and 4 in math.	3	52
Schools Identified 2009-10 (On probation 2009-10 year; trend data: 2006-07 to 2008-09)	226	READING 4; Math 3 READING 5; Math 3 Out of 6 test trend patterns in reading and 6 in math.	2 1	19 20

FIGURE C.1

Group-based trajectories of schools on probation as predicted by the reading and math scores

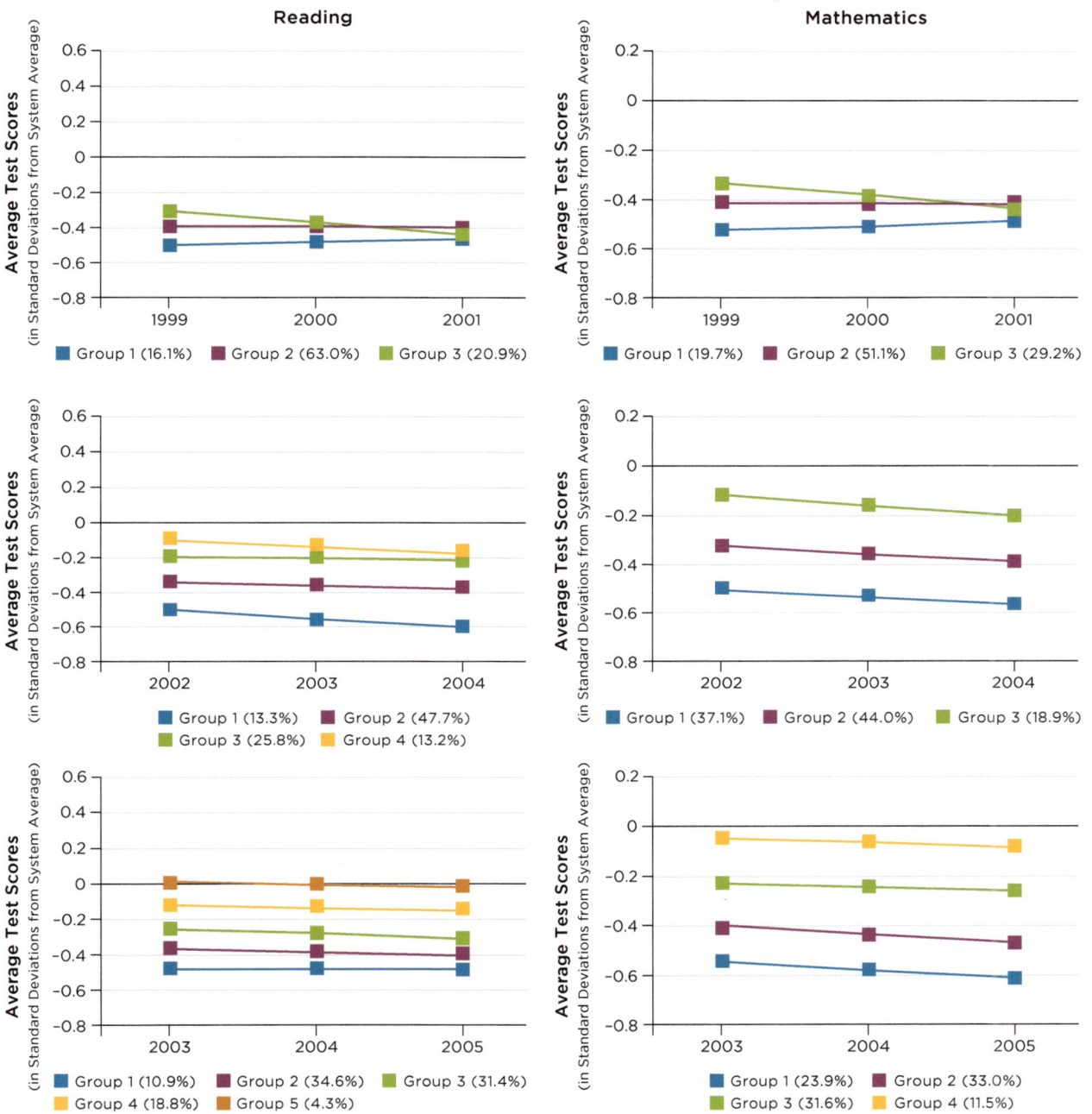

Note: Numbers in parentheses represent the percentage of schools in each group.

Appendix C

FIGURE C.1 *CONTINUED*

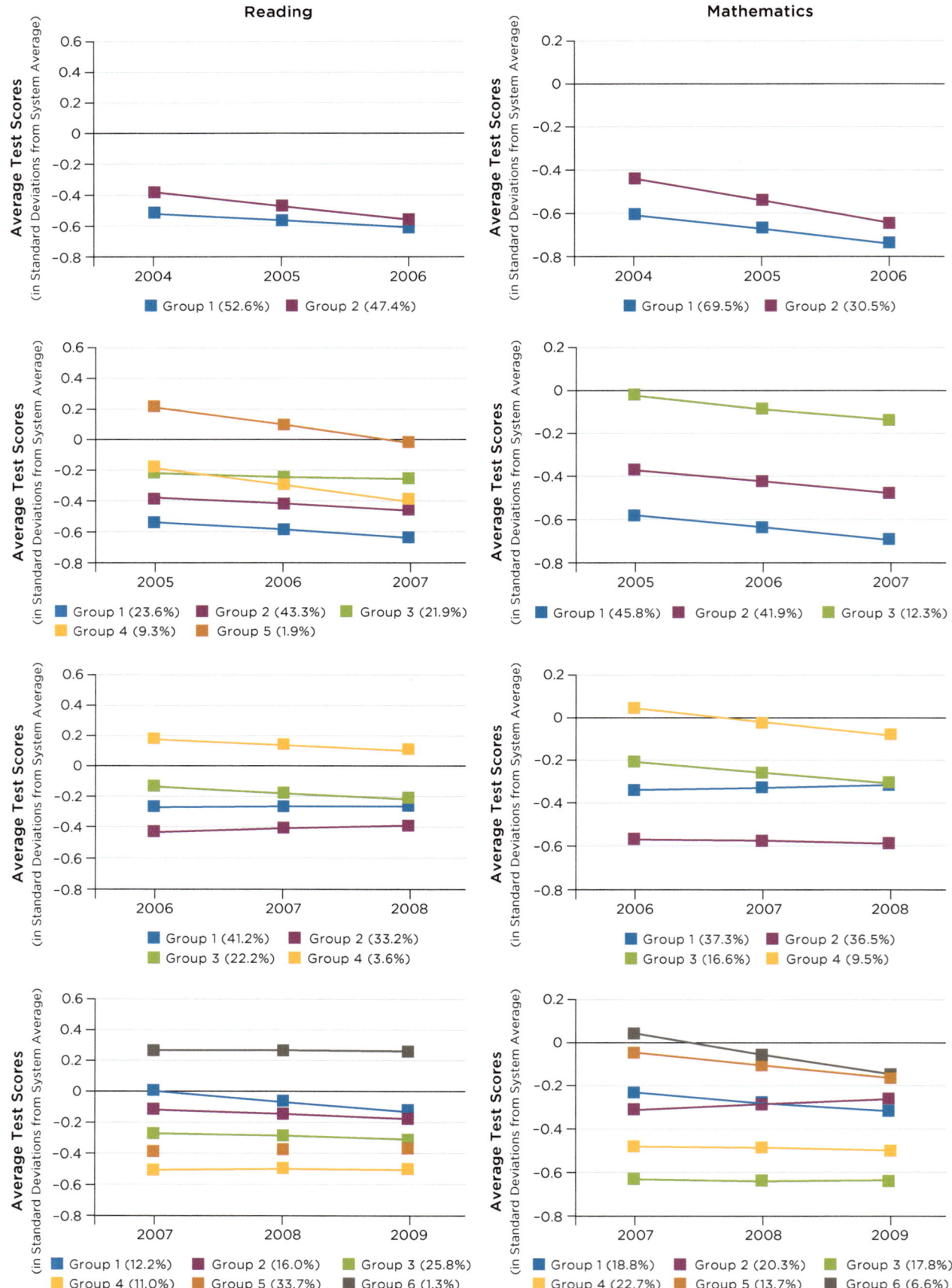

Propensity Score Analysis

We used the trajectory information along with propensity scores to find the best possible matches for the intervention schools. Treated schools were matched to a comparison group of schools on the basis of a series of school-level characteristics observed in the academic year prior to the decision by the district to intervene. For example, in the case of Dodge and Williams, which were closed at the end of the 2001-02 academic year, propensity score models were based on characteristics of schools in the 2000-01 academic year. This corresponds to the data the district would have used to make decisions about intervening.

The school characteristics included in the propensity score analysis were school racial composition, percentage of students with limited English proficiency, percentage of students receiving special education services, percentage of students receiving free or reduced-priced lunch, attendance, mobility, percentage of students who were truant, the average concentration of poverty (male unemployment and percentage of families living under the poverty line) and social status (years of education and employment as managers or executives) in the census blocks where students reside, and the size of the school. In addition, reading and math scores for the past three years, and probation status in the prior three years, were included in the construction of propensity scores. Because in most time periods only one or two schools were identified for intervention, data for all periods were pooled for the propensity analysis with dummy variables indicating the various time frames. Two potential comparison schools had missing data on mobility and truancy and were dropped from the analysis; the final sample size was 964 schools. **Table C.5** shows information on the treated and untreated schools on all the covariates included in the propensity analysis. Elementary schools that underwent intervention, in comparison with other schools on probation in the intervention year that were not selected for intervention, had lower average test scores and attendance, had higher mobility rates, and served students who tended to come from neighborhoods with higher levels of poverty. Treatment schools also were more likely to have been on probation during the year prior to intervention and the year before that (two years prior).

Several approaches to matching the treatment and control schools were tested to ensure that the conclusions were not affected by the choice of methodology. All matches were based on the logit of the propensity score, and only schools with the same reading and math group trajectories as the treated school were considered as appropriate matches.[55] Matching was done through the following three approaches: Nearest neighbor, caliper, and estimated propensity as weights. Each has advantages and disadvantages. The nearest neighbor approach ensures that all treated schools are included in the analysis; with this approach, the school with the closest propensity score is selected as the control. The caliper approach ensures that all comparison schools have a similar propensity for treatment as the treated schools; schools are considered to be a potential match only if their logit propensity score falls within 0.2 standard deviations of the treated school. Up to two schools are allowed to be picked as controls for each treated school.[56] This approach eliminates bad matches when the closest match to a treated school is far away, but it can reduce the number of treated schools included in the analysis. With both the nearest neighbor and the caliper matching approaches, only a few schools from the control group are used to estimate the counterfactual outcome; therefore, the standard error of the estimate is higher than in the case where more information is included. We used a third approach, propensity score weighting, to include information from a larger comparison group. In this approach, we used all potential control schools—those on probation within the same trajectory group—and weighted those schools by (propensity score/[1-propensity score]) for the analysis.[57] The treated schools get a weight of 1 in the analysis. This method allows us to obtain a balanced sample of treated and control schools using more schools from the control group.

Table C.5 displays information for elementary schools on each variable included in the model for (1) the treated schools, (2) all untreated, possible control schools, and (3) the comparison schools chosen on the basis of each of the three matching approaches. Although differences in the observable variables exist between the treated and untreated schools, all differences in observables but one, average social status,

TABLE C.5

Mean values and differences on observed variables for elementary school comparison groups

Variables	Treated Schools (N = 22) Mean	Untreated Schools (possible control schools) (N = 964) Difference	Matched Schools, Nearest Neighbor Approach (N = 22) Difference	Matched Schools, Caliper Approach (N = 30) 17 Treated Schools Matched Difference	Propensity-Weighted Approach (N = 245) Difference
Reading Score Three Years Prior	-0.45	0.19***	0.00	0.00	0.00
Reading Score Two Years Prior	-0.49	0.21***	0.01	0.02	0.01
Reading Score the Year Prior to Intervention	-0.52	0.22***	0.01	0.02	-0.02
Math Score Three Years Prior	-0.51	0.21***	0.02	0.00	0.00
Math Score Two Years Prior	-0.56	0.23***	0.03	-0.01	-0.01
Math Score the Year Prior to Intervention	-0.61	0.25***	0.04	0.01	0.00
Percentage African American	0.95	-0.14-	-0.01	-0.02	0.01
Percentage Latino	0.05	0.12-	0.01	0.01	-0.01
Percentage White	0.00	0.01	0.00	0.00	0.00
Percentage Asian American	0.00	0.00	0.00	0.00	0.00
Percentage LEP	0.01	0.06*	0.02	0.01	0.01
Percentage IEP	0.11	0.01	0.01	0.01	0.01
Percentage Low-Income	0.95	-0.02	-0.03-	0.00	-0.01-
Percentage Attendance	0.91	0.02***	0.00	0.00	0.00
Mobility	0.41	-0.09*	-0.02	-0.03	-0.02
Percentage Truant	0.09	-0.04*	0.00	0.02	-0.02-
Neighborhood Concentration of Poverty	1.09	-0.35***	-0.16	-0.13	-0.03
Neighborhood Social Status	-0.58	0.13	0.20*	0.10	0.08*
On Probation Three Years Prior to Intervention	0.59	-0.20-	0.14	0.14	0.03
On Probation Two Years Prior to Intervention	0.82	-0.41***	-0.14	-0.12	0.00
On Probation the Year Prior to Intervention	0.95	-0.34***	-0.09	-0.04	-0.04
School Size (× 100)	5.19	0.63	1.05	0.47	-0.16
Propensity Score	0.18	-0.16***	-0.04	-0.01	0.01

Note: Differences from treated schools are significant at -p < 0.10, *p < 0.05, **p < 0.01, and ***p < 0.001.

become statistically insignificant after matching the treated schools with the nearest neighbor approach. When caliper matching was done, five schools could not be matched because their propensities for treatment were substantially higher than any untreated school. Therefore, 17 treatment schools were compared to 30 matched schools in the caliper matching analysis, and differences in all of the observed variables become statistically insignificant, compared to the treated schools. The propensity weighting approach balances all the covariates but one, the average social status of the neighborhoods where students enrolled in these schools lived.

Statistical Models for Analyzing Outcomes

To examine the impact of turnaround efforts, we ran analyses that contrasted student achievement before and after intervention, and contrasted these with in-school differences, in control versus treatment schools. For elementary schools, we used three-level hierarchical models, with students nested within years nested within schools. This analysis model allows schools to be compared to their own prior achievement levels, showing changes in test scores in the years after intervention in comparison with the years prior to intervention. The comparison schools provide a further contrast—a difference-in-differences approach—to ensure that the patterns observed in the treated schools are not also observed in schools that were not treated. This might occur, for example, if there were system-wide changes in test scores, or if test forms were not well equated over time. The models discern changes in test scores that were above and beyond any changes observed in the comparison schools.

The models also included student-level covariates to adjust for any changes in the types of students who were attending the schools over the period being analyzed. These covariates were group-mean-centered at the school level, around the mean levels of each school across all years included in the analysis.[58]

Thus, the model shows the average test scores adjusted for changes in the types of students in the school, in comparison with the intervention year. Besides adjusting for student background, the level-1 models included dummy variables for grade level. These variables adjust for grade-level differences.

Variables were included at level-2 (time) to discern differences in the rate of test-score improvements before and after the intervention. One variable, TREND, discerned the rate of change in test scores prior to the intervention—coded as 0 in the year prior to intervention, and -1 and -2 in the years before that. A dummy variable, STERM, discerned any change in test scores in the first year of the intervention (which was coded zero under TREND). A third variable, MTREND, measured the yearly trend in test score growth in the years after the intervention (coded as 0 until the first year of intervention and coded as 1, 2, 3, and so forth in each subsequent year). One more variable, LTREND, was included to discern long-term trends in schools that had been under reform for more than four years. Few schools had enough data to contribute to this term, so this variable is included only so that long-term trends in a few schools do not bias the estimates of the midterm trends across all the schools. **Table C.6** lists the numbers of elementary schools selected for intervention with available data for the estimation of the various trend estimates.

Finally, a dummy variable, ANN_YR, was included to indicate the year that the announcement took place for the intervention schools (coded 1 for the year of the announcement for schools that underwent intervention, 0 otherwise) to control for negative effects associated with this event. **Table C.7** provides the coding for these five variables.

At level-3 (school level), dummy variables identified differences between treated and comparison schools. Differences were discerned for coefficients representing average test scores during intervention year (intercept, β_{00}); the yearly test score trend prior to intervention (β_{01}); average test scores in first intervention year (β_{02}); and the yearly test score trend during the first four years of the intervention (β_{04}).

TABLE C.6

Number of treatment elementary schools with available data to estimate growth parameters

Parameter	Number of Treatment Schools
TREND	22
STERM	22
MTREND (at least two years after intervention)	19
LTREND (at least five years after intervention)	9

TABLE C.7

Coding of level-2 variables

	Before Intervention				After Intervention						
	Year 4	Year 3	Year 2	Year 1	Year 1	Year 2	Year 3	Year 4	Year 5	Year 6	Year 7
TREND	-3	-2	-1	0	0	0	0	0	0	0	0
STERM	0	0	0	0	1	1	1	1	1	1	1
MTREND	0	0	0	0	0	1	2	3	4	5	6
LTREND	0	0	0	0	0	0	0	0	1	2	3
ANN_YR	0	0	0	1	0	0	0	0	0	0	0

The models for reading and math scores for elementary schools are specified as follows:

LEVEL-1 MODEL

Students

$$\text{Z-SCORE}_{ijk} = \pi_{0jk} + \pi_{1jk}*(GR3_{ijk}) + \pi_{2jk}*(GR5_{ijk}) + \pi_{3jk}*(GR6_{ijk}) + \pi_{4jk}*(GR7_{ijk}) + \pi_{5jk}*(GR8_{ijk}) + \pi_{6jk}*(\text{previous test score}_{ijk}) + \pi_{7jk}*(\text{previous test score}^2_{ijk}) + \pi_{8jk}*(\text{male}_{ijk}) + \pi_{9jk}*(\text{white}_{ijk}) + \pi_{10jk}*(\text{Asian American}_{ijk}) + \pi_{11jk}*(\text{Latino}_{ijk}) + \pi_{12jk}*(\text{special education}_{ijk}) + \pi_{13jk}*(\text{old for grade}_{ijk}) + \pi_{14jk}*(\text{neighborhood concentration of poverty}_{ijk}) + \pi_{15jk}*(\text{neighborhood social status}_{ijk}) + \pi_{16jk}*(\text{limited English proficent}_{ijk}) + e_{ijk}$$

LEVEL-2 MODEL

Time

$$\pi_{0jk} = \beta_{00k} + \beta_{01k}*(TREND_{jk}) + \beta_{02k}*(STERM_{jk}) + \beta_{03k}*(MTREND_{jk}) + \beta_{04k}*(LTREND_{jk}) + \beta_{05k}*(ANN\_YR_{jk}) + r_{0jk}$$
$$\pi_{ajk} = \beta_{a0k}, \text{ for } a = 1 \text{ to } 16$$

LEVEL-3 MODEL

Schools

$$\beta_{00k} = \gamma_{000} + \gamma_{001}(TREATED_k) + u_{00k}$$
$$\beta_{01k} = \gamma_{010} + \gamma_{011}(TREATED_k) + u_{01k}$$
$$\beta_{02k} = \gamma_{020} + \gamma_{021}(TREATED_k) + u_{02k}$$
$$\beta_{03k} = \gamma_{030} + \gamma_{031}(TREATED_k) + u_{03k}$$
$$\beta_{04k} = \gamma_{040} + \gamma_{041}(TREATED_k) + u_{04k}$$
$$\beta_{05k} = \gamma_{050}$$
$$\beta_{a0k} = \gamma_{a00} \text{ for } a = 1 \text{ to } 16$$

Tables C.8 and C.9 show the different estimation steps until the final models described above were estimated for reading and math scores. The estimates show that the estimates of interest, the treated differences in the intercept, TREND, STERM, and MTREND, are very stable in all different steps. The introduction of student covariates reduces the magnitude of the treated difference in MTREND, but it is still statistically significant.

TABLE C.8

Estimates for reading test scores; different models and different propensity score matching methods

	Nearest Neighbor						Caliper	Propensity Weighting
	No Student Covariates; Only u_{00k} Included	No Student Covariates; u_{00k} and u_{01k} Included	No Student Covariates; u_{00k}, u_{01k}, and u_{02k} Included	No Student Covariates; u_{00k}, u_{01k}, u_{02k}, and u_{03k} Included	No Student Covariates; Full Model	With Student Covariates; Full Model	With Student Covariates; Full Model	With Student Covariates; Full Model
Intercept	-0.460***	-0.459***	-0.460***	-0.460***	-0.460***	-0.457***	-0.459***	-0.477***
Treated Difference	0.024	0.024	0.022	0.023	0.022	-0.004	0.001	0.032
Pre-Intervention TREND	-0.002	-0.002	-0.002	-0.002	-0.002	-0.002	-0.010	-0.013*
Treated Difference	-0.036-	-0.035	-0.036*	-0.036*	-0.036*	-0.019	-0.015	-0.007
First Year of Intervention (STERM)	0.035	0.036	0.038	0.035	0.036	0.004	0.036-	0.029-
Treated Difference	0.045	0.046	0.055	0.045	0.043	0.052	0.016	0.031
Trendin First Four Years (MTREND)	-0.002	0.000	0.005	0.013	-0.011	-0.001	0.001	0.000
Treated Difference	0.087***	0.081***	0.069***	0.075***	0.079***	0.050**	0.052**	0.050*
Later Trend (LTREND)	-0.052*	-0.059*	-0.068**	0.068**	-0.086**	-0.065*	-0.013	-0.017
Treated Difference	0.008	0.007	0.013	-0.017	-0.078*	-0.049	-0.113*	-0.075-
Announcement Year	0.036	0.037	0.038	0.038	0.038	0.032	0.035	0.031
Grade 3	-0.004	-0.004	-0.005	-0.005	-0.005	0.100***	0.087***	0.154***
Grade 5	-0.034***	-0.034***	-0.035***	-0.035***	-0.035***	0.086***	0.093***	0.081***
Grade 6	-0.002	-0.010	-0.002	-0.002	-0.035***	0.182***	0.168***	0.183***
Grade 7	-0.010	-0.002	-0.011	-0.011	-0.002	0.111***	0.100***	0.117***
Grade 8	-0.002	-0.010	-0.001	-0.002	-0.011	0.167***	0.164***	0.174***
Prior Reading Score						0.473***	0.475***	0.480***
Prior Reading Score (Squared)						-0.003	-0.002	-0.002
Male Student						-0.089***	-0.089***	-0.087***
White Student						0.055	0.062	0.058
Asian American Student						0.240*	0.157	0.190
Latino Student						0.097***	0.163***	0.101*
Student With IEP						-0.579***	-0.599***	-0.578***
Student Old for Grade						-0.170***	-0.179***	-0.174***
Neighborhood Concentration of Poverty						-0.032***	-0.023***	-0.030*
Neighborhood Social Status						0.004	0.007**	0.001
LEP						-0.456***	-0.517***	-0.453***
Variance Components								
e_{ijk}	0.75968	0.75969	0.75970	0.75967	0.75967	0.42916	0.43000	0.42746
r_{0jk}	0.00971**	0.00696**	0.00439***	0.00337***	0.00327***	0.00377***	0.00380***	0.00487***
u_{00k}	0.01165***	0.01108***	0.01114***	0.01136***	0.01136***	0.01039***	0.00702***	0.01064***
u_{01k}		0.00188***	0.00014	0.00034*	0.00036	0.00025**	0.00016**	0.00020***
u_{02k}			0.01520***	0.00847***	0.00927***	0.00276**	0.00150*	0.00444***
u_{03k}				0.00124***	0.00124***	0.00063**	0.00010**	0.00118*
u_{04k}					0.00301***	0.00296	0.00201**	0.00574**
Number of Observations								
Students	117,404	117,404	117,404	117,404	117,404	85,360	92,905	542,404
Schools	44 22 Treated, 22 Control	44 22 Treated, 22 Control	44 22 Treated, 22 Control	44 22 Treated, 22 Control	44 22 Treated, 22 Control	44 22 Treated, 22 Control	47 17 Treated, 30 Control	267 22 Treated, 245 Control

Note: Significance: -$p < 0.10$, *$p < 0.05$, **$p < 0.01$, and ***$p < 0.001$

TABLE C.9

Estimates for math test scores outcome; different models and different propensity score matching methods

	Nearest Neighbor						Caliper	Propensity Weighting
	No Student Covariates; Only u_{00k} Included	No Student Covariates; u_{00k} and u_{01k} Included	No Student Covariates; u_{00k}, u_{01k}, and u_{02k} Included	No Student Covariates; u_{00k}, u_{01k}, u_{02k}, and u_{03k} Included	No Student Covariates; Full Model	With Student Covariates; Full Model	With Student Covariates; Full Model	With Student Covariates; Full Model
Intercept	-0.532***	-0.533***	-0.535***	-0.536***	-0.536***	-0.524***	-0.536***	-0.539***
Treated Difference	0.041	0.042	0.041	0.043	0.022	-0.005	0.022	0.043
Pre-Intervention TREND	-0.015	-0.014	-0.016	-0.016-	-0.016-	-0.012	-0.014-	-0.014*
Treated Difference	-0.036	-0.037	-0.035-	-0.035*	-0.035*	-0.020	-0.029-	-0.016
First Year of Intervention (STERM)	0.023	0.025	0.031	0.023	0.022	-0.009	0.038	0.042*
Treated Difference	**0.137***	**0.134***	**0.130-**	**0.116***	**0.116***	**0.104***	**0.121***	**0.081**
Trend in First Four Years (MTREND)	0.006	-0.013	0.024*	0.048*	0.049*	0.016	0.047**	0.032***
Treated Difference	**0.085***	**0.085***	**0.083***	**0.098***	**0.098***	**0.062***	**0.027***	**0.053***
Later Trend (LTREND)	-0.042	-0.055-	-0.071**	-0.044*	-0.086 **	-0.110**	-0.006	-0.028
Treated Difference	0.003	0.000	-0.001	-0.052	-0.068*	-0.045**	-0.050*	-0.069
Announcement Year	0.044	0.044	0.043	0.041	0.041	0.043	0.600	0.043
Grade 3	-0.018*	-0.018*	-0.018*	-0.018*	-0.018*	0.110***	0.076***	0.129***
Grade 5	-0.022**	-0.022**	-0.022**	-0.022**	-0.022**	0.112***	0.100***	0.099***
Grade 6	0.004	0.004	0.004	0.003	0.003	0.172***	0.146***	0.170***
Grade 7	-0.007	-0.007	-0.007	-0.007	-0.007	0.124***	0.098***	0.126***
Grade 8	-0.010	-0.010	-0.011	-0.011	-0.011	0.183***	0.163***	0.175***
Prior Math Score						0.498***	0.485***	0.501***
Prior Math Score (Squared)						-0.017***	-0.024***	-0.016**
Male Student						-0.015***	-0.017***	-0.011
White Student						0.091*	0.160**	0.114
Asian American Student						0.300**	0.292*	0.325
Latino Student						0.138***	0.197***	0.173***
Student With IEP						-0.449***	-0.452***	-0.434***
Student Old for Grade						-0.124***	-0.143*	-0.134***
Neighborhood Concentration of Poverty						-0.019***	-0.012**	-0.016
Neighborhood Social Status						0.002	0.007	0.001
LEP						-0.353***	-0.466***	-0.332***
Variance Components								
e_{ijk}	0.65388	0.65390	0.65393	0.65386	0.65387	0.35369	0.35620	0.35208
r_{0jk}	0.01882***	0.01412***	0.00875***	0.00406***	0.00401***	0.00653***	0.00624***	0.00661***
u_{00k}	0.01388***	0.01410***	0.01462***	0.01537***	0.01538***	0.01653***	0.00785***	0.01419***
u_{01k}		0.00327***	0.00031	0.00078**	0.00079**	0.00030**	0.00013	0.00053***
u_{02k}			0.02948***	0.01223***	0.01153***	0.00245	0.00364	0.00576**
u_{03k}				0.00748***	0.00824***	0.00138	0.00238*	0.00136
u_{04k}					0.00508-	0.00456	0.00406	0.00101
Number of Observations								
Students	117,146	117,146	117,146	117,146	117,146	84,756	92,218	538,457
Schools	44; 22 Treated, 22 Control	44; 22 Treated, 22 Control	44; 22 Treated, 22 Control	44; 22 Treated, 22 Control	44; 22 Treated, 22 Control	44; 22 Treated, 22 Control	47; 17 Treated, 30 Control	267; 22 Treated, 245 Control

Note: Significance: -p < 0.10, *p < 0.05, **p < 0.01, and ***p < 0.001

Sensitivity Analysis

Although the MTREND estimates for reading and STERM and MTREND for math scores are fairly robust to different models and matching strategies, it is possible that selection on unobserved covariates could explain the statistically significant effects. We now explore this possibility using the techniques described in Rosenbaum (2002). The idea behind this sensitivity analysis is to determine how strongly an unmeasured variable must influence selection to be able to explain the effects on the coefficients that are statistically significant.

Imagine that two schools that look the same before intervention in the observed covariates may be different in terms of unobserved covariates. So one school might be $\Gamma \geq 1$ times as likely to be selected to undergo intervention as the matched school because of an unobserved covariate. The sensitivity analysis provides a way to test the null hypothesis of no effect from such unobserved variable for different values of Γ. **Table C.10** shows the ranges of p-values for the null hypothesis of no effect for values of Γ. Only a large bias (Γ greater than 5) could explain the statistically significant results estimated for MTREND in reading and for STERM and MTREND in math.

TABLE C.10
Sensitivity analysis for estimates of trend in the first four years (MTREND) in reading and math

	Reading		Math			
	MTREND		STERM		MTREND	
	Pmin	Pmax	Pmin	Pmax	Pmin	Pmax
$\Gamma = 1$	<0.001	<0.001	<0.001	<0.001	<0.001	<0.001
$\Gamma = 2$	<0.001	0.003	<0.001	0.002	<0.001	0.003
$\Gamma = 3$	<0.001	0.014	<0.001	0.009	<0.001	0.014
$\Gamma = 4$	<0.001	0.028	<0.001	0.020	<0.001	0.028
$\Gamma = 5$	<0.001	0.044	<0.001	0.033	<0.001	0.044

Analyses on Grade 9-12 Absences and Grade 9 On-Track to Graduate Rates

Our strategy to estimate the effect of the intervention on absence rates and on-track to graduate rates for high schools relied on a difference-in-differences design, similar to the elementary school analysis. Student absence rates were recorded by CPS slightly differently in the years prior to 2007-08 than in the years after. In addition, only absences in the fall semester are available for one of the years, a year in which there was a change in the student information system. In order to make measures comparable, we converted each student's absence rate into standard deviations from the system mean for each fall semester and grade. This makes the measure of absence rates consistent across all the years included in this study; they can be interpreted as the degree to which students' absence rates for the fall semester were different from the average in the system for that year and grade. Standardizing within year also adjusts for any system wide trends that should not be attributed to the interventions. The on-track to graduate variable was not standardized because it was measured in the same way for all years in the study.[59]

The steps for analysis of high school outcomes were similar to the elementary school analysis. The first step consisted of identifying a plausible comparison group for intervention schools that were not identified for turnaround interventions. Group-based trajectory analysis was used along with propensity score analysis to select a sample of comparison schools. This allowed selecting comparison schools that had similar patterns in the outcome variables in the prior years leading up to intervention and also had similar school characteristics based on the composition of students.

Sample

The sample of high schools that underwent intervention were all low-performing schools on probation the year the district decided to intervene. As with elementary schools, comparison schools included only schools that were on probation in the year the treated schools were identified for intervention. Again, we restricted the pool of potential comparison schools to those that were in existence for at least four years prior to the year the treated schools underwent intervention. **Table C.11** shows the number of schools that were on probation during the years the schools in the treatment group were identified for intervention and that had at least three years of test scores before that year. The 14 high schools that underwent intervention were not included as potential matching schools, even if they were on probation during periods prior to or subsequent to their own reform.

Group-Based Trajectory Analysis

Group-based trajectory analyses for the five time periods were conducted separately for absences and on-track rates using SAS and the latent class procedure *proc traj*. Model selection criteria were similar to those used for elementary schools. The trajectory information ensured that schools were not only similar in their outcome measure right before the intervention but had also been on similar trends prior to intervention. **Figure C.2** displays the trajectories and groups for high schools. **See Table C.11** for a description of eligible schools within each intervention period, the number of patterns observed within each period, which patterns the intervened schools were in, and the number of potential control schools to be used in the final hierarchical analyses.

Propensity Score Analysis

As with elementary schools, we used the trajectory information along with propensity scores to find the best possible matches for the intervention schools. Treated schools were matched to a comparison group of schools on the basis of a series of school-level characteristics observed in the academic year prior to the decision by the district to intervene (**see Appendix B** for a description of the variables). The final sample size for high schools was 234 schools.

Table C.12 shows information on treated and untreated high schools on all covariates included in propensity analysis. Except for the proportion of Asian American students in the school and the percentage of low-income students in the school, the treated high schools are significantly different from the comparison schools on all covariates included in the propensity analysis. Matching was done through the three approaches: *nearest neighbor, caliper,* and *estimated propensity as weights*. **Table C.12** displays the matching information for high schools on each covariate included in the model for (1) the treated schools; (2) all untreated, possible control schools; and (3) the comparison schools chosen on the basis of each of the three matching approaches. In order to find balance in the observed variables when using the nearest neighbor matching technique, we had to allow for matching with replacement. The 14 high schools are matched to 10 comparison schools; the two groups are similar on all observed variables, except in the size of the school. Caliper matching for high school discerned matches for only six treated schools, with seven schools falling within the caliper ranges of those six schools. With this method, all the covariates are balanced although the sample size is reduced considerably. Propensity weighting balances all but five (absences three year prior, percentage of students with IEPs, percentage of low-income students, the average social capital of the students, and the size of the school) of the observed variables.

TABLE C.11
High schools that matched selection criteria to be in the comparison group

Intervention Period	Number of Schools on Probation	Number of Observed Test Trend Patterns	Absences and On-Track Trend Patterns of Intervention Schools	Number of Possible Control Schools in Same Absences and On-Track Trend Groups
Schools Identified 1996-97 (On probation 1996-97 year; trend data: 1993-94 to 1995-96)	35	ABSENCES 1; ON-TRACK 1	1	3
		ABSENCES 2; ON-TRACK 1	3	3
		ABSENCES 2; ON-TRACK 2	2	4
		ABSENCES 3; ON-TRACK 1	1	1
		Out of 3 trend patterns in absences and 2 in on-track.		
Schools Identified 2004-05 (On probation 2004-05 year; trend data: 2001-02 to 2003-04)	39	ABSENCES 4; ON-TRACK 2 Out of 4 trend patterns in absences and 2 in on-track.	1	3
Schools Identified 2005-06 (On probation 2005-06 year; trend data: 2002-03 to 2004-05)	36	ABSENCES 4; ON-TRACK 2 Out of 4 trend patterns in absences and 3 in on-track.	1	2
Schools Identified 2007-08 (On probation 2007-08 year; trend data: 2004-05 to 2006-07)	40	ABSENCES 1; ON-TRACK 1	1	11
		ABSENCES 2; ON-TRACK 1	1	9
		Out of 3 trend patterns in absences and 2 in on-track.		
Schools Identified 2008-09 (On probation 2008-09 year; trend data: 2005-06 to 2007-08)	48	ABSENCES 4; ON-TRACK 1 Out of 4 trend patterns in absences and 2 in on-track.	1	2
Schools Identified 2009-10 (On probation 2009-10 year; trend data: 2006-07 to 2008-09)	52	ABSENCES 2; ON-TRACK 1 Out of 2 trend patterns in absences and 2 in on-track.	2	22

FIGURE C.2

Group-based trajectory of schools on probation as predicted by the absences and on-track to graduate rates

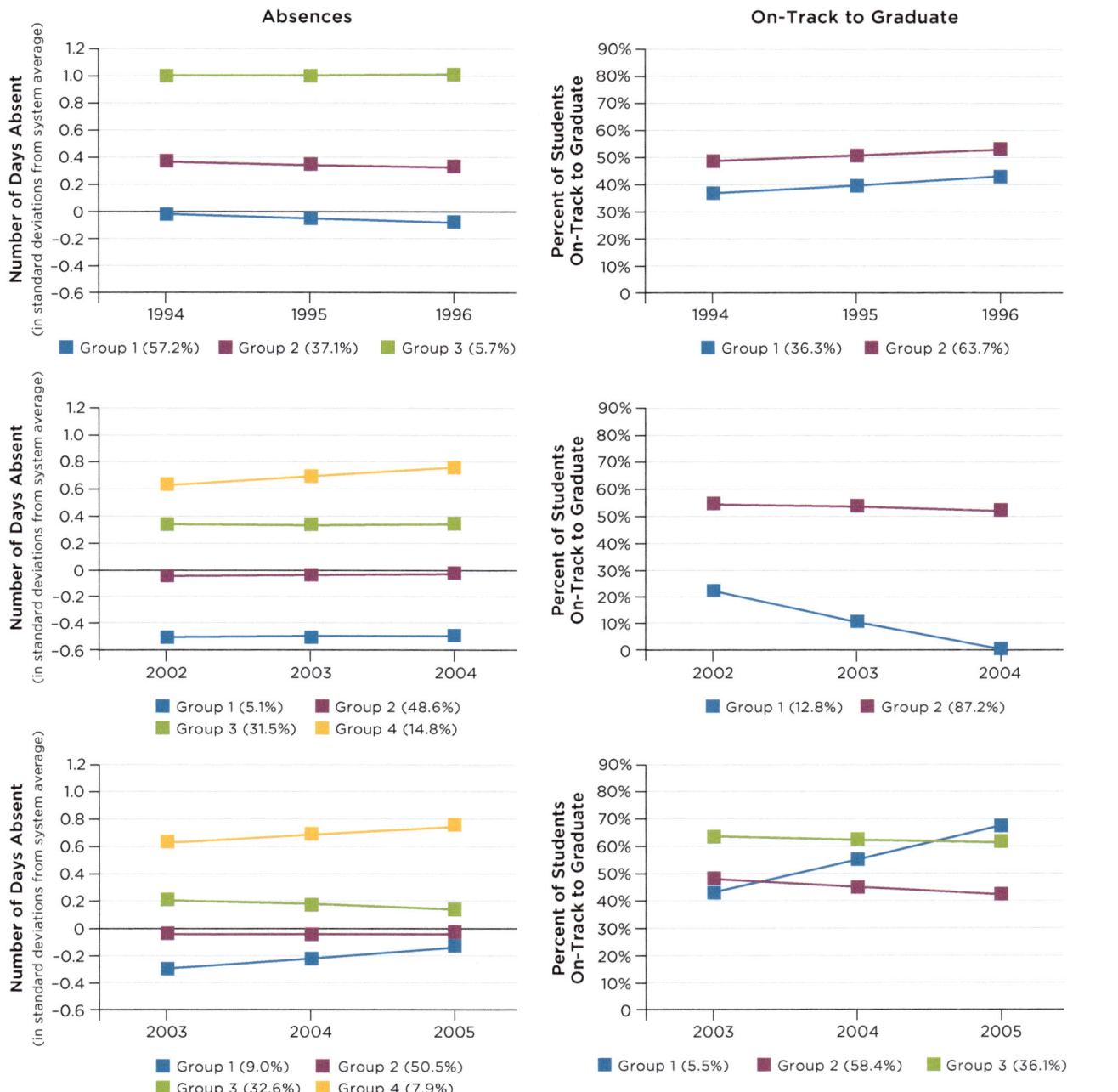

Note: Numbers in parentheses represent the percentage of schools in each group.

Appendix C

FIGURE C.2 CONTINUED

Group-based trajectory of schools on probation as predicted by the absences and on-track to graduate rates

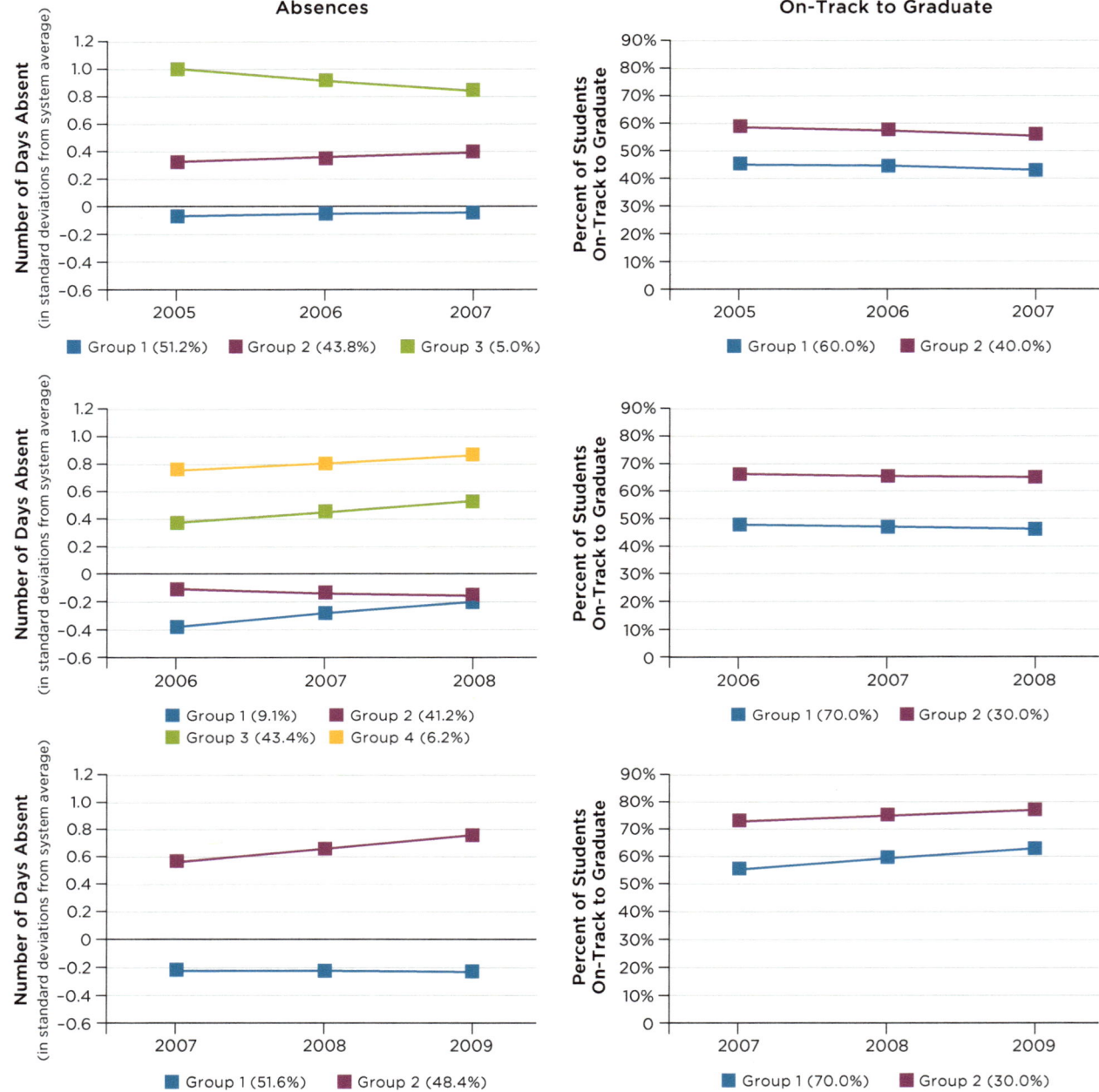

Note: Numbers in parentheses represent the percentage of schools in each group.

TABLE C.12
Mean values and differences on observed variables for high school comparison groups

Variables	Treated Schools (N = 14) Mean	Untreated Schools (possible control schools) (N = 234) Difference	Matched Schools, Nearest Neighbor Approach (N = 10) Difference	Matched Schools, Caliper Approach (N = 7) 6 Treated Schools Matched Difference	Propensity-Weighted Approach (N = 60) Difference
Absences Three Years Prior	0.50	-0.40***	-0.04	-0.004	-0.13*
Absences Two Years Prior	0.51	-0.40***	-0.08	-0.19	-0.04
Absences One Year Prior	0.45	-0.322*	0.05	-0.09	0.01
On-Track Three Years Prior	0.39	0.15***	0.02	0.05	-0.01
On-Track Two Years Prior	0.41	0.12***	0.01	0.03	-0.03
On-Track One Year Prior	0.41	0.13***	0.01	0.01	-0.03
Math Comp	-0.55	0.17***	0.08	0.07	0.01
Reading Comp	-0.56	0.21***	0.04	0.04	0.01
Percentage African American	0.99	-0.40***	-0.10	-0.09	-0.03
Percentage Latino	0.01	0.33***	0.09-	0.08	0.02
Percentage Asian American	0.00	0.02	0.00	0.01	0.00
Percentage LEP	0.00	0.07**	0.03-	0.02	0.01
Percentage IEP	0.21	-0.04*	-0.01	-0.03	-0.02**
Percentage Low-Income	0.86	0.01	0.03	0.03	0.04*
Mobility	0.49	-0.20***	-0.03	-0.11	0.00
Percentage Truant	0.27	-0.12**	-0.04	-0.11	-0.02
Percentage Dropout	0.22	-0.09***	-0.03	-0.04	-0.01
Neighborhood Concentration of Poverty	0.98	-0.62***	0.06	-0.02	0.03
Neighborhood Social Status	-0.53	0.14	-0.06	0.12	-0.11**
Size, Grade 9 (x100)	5.42	-0.94	-1.50*	-1.81	-1.58***
Propensity Score	0.52	-0.49***	-0.16	-0.11	0.11

Note: Differences from treated schools are significant at -p < 0.10, *p < 0.05, **p < 0.01, and ***p < 0.001.

Statistical Models for Analyzing High School Outcomes

To examine the impact of turnaround efforts for high schools, we ran analyses that contrasted student outcomes before and after intervention both in control and in treatment schools.

The models for high schools are specified very similarly to the elementary school models. One important difference is that for on-track to graduate rates, the outcome being binary, the model used was a logistic three-level hierarchical linear model.

The model for high school absences is specified as follows:

LEVEL-1 MODEL

$ZABSENT_{ijk} = \pi_{0jk} + \pi_{1jk}*(\text{reading score eighth grade}_{ijk}) + \pi_{2jk}*(\text{male}_{ijk}) + \pi_{3jk}*(\text{white}_{ijk}) + \pi_{4jk}*(\text{Latino}_{ijk}) + \pi_{5jk}*(\text{Asian American}_{ijk}) + \pi_{6jk}*(\text{special education}_{ijk}) + \pi_{7jk}*(\text{old for grade}_{ijk}) + \pi_{8jk}*(\text{neighborhood concentration of poverty}_{ijk}) + \pi_{9jk}*(\text{neighborhood social status}_{ijk}) + \pi_{10jk}*(\text{grade10}_{ijk}) + \pi_{11jk}*(\text{grade11}_{ijk}) + \pi_{12jk}*(\text{grade12}_{ijk}) + e_{ijk}$

LEVEL-2 MODEL

$\pi_{0jk} = \beta_{00k} + \beta_{01k}*(TREND_{jk}) + \beta_{02k}*(STERM_{jk}) + \beta_{03k}*(MTREND_{jk}) + \beta_{04k}*(LTREND_{jk}) + \beta_{05k}*(ANN\_YR_{jk}) + r_{0jk}$
$\pi_{ajk} = \beta_{a0k}$ for a = 1 to 12

LEVEL-3 MODEL

$\beta_{00k} = \gamma_{000} + \gamma_{001}(TREATEDk) + u_{00k}$
$\beta_{01k} = \gamma_{010} + \gamma_{011}(TREATEDk) + u_{01k}$
$\beta_{02k} = \gamma_{020} + \gamma_{021}(TREATEDk) + u_{02k}$
$\beta_{03k} = \gamma_{030} + \gamma_{031}(TREATEDk) + u_{03k}$
$\beta_{04k} = \gamma_{040} + \gamma_{041}(TREATEDk) + u_{04k}$
$\beta_{05k} = \gamma_{050}$
$\beta_{a0k} = \gamma_{a00}$ for a = 1 to 12

The statistical model for on-track to graduate is specified as follows:

LEVEL-1 MODEL

$Prob(ONTRACK_{ijk}=1|\pi_{jk}) = \phi_{ijk}$
$\log[\phi_{ijk}/(1 - \phi_{ijk})] = \eta_{ijk}$
$\eta_{ijk} = \pi_{0jk} + \pi_{1jk}*(\text{reading score eighth grade}_{ijk}) + \pi_{2jk}*(\text{male}_{ijk}) + \pi_{3jk}*(\text{white}_{ijk}) + \pi_{4jk}*(\text{Latino}_{ijk}) + \pi_{5jk}*(\text{Asian American}_{ijk}) + \pi_{6jk}*(\text{special education}_{ijk}) + \pi_{7jk}*(\text{old for grade}_{ijk}) + \pi_{8jk}*(\text{neighborhood concentration of poverty}_{ijk}) + \pi_{9jk}*(\text{neighborhood social status}_{ijk})$

LEVEL-2 MODEL

$$\pi_{0jk} = \beta_{00k} + \beta_{01k}*(TREND_{jk}) + \beta_{02k}*(STERM_{jk}) + \beta_{03k}*(MTREND_{jk}) + \beta_{04k}*(LTREND_{jk}) + \beta_{05k}*(ANN\_YR_{jk}) + r_{0jk}$$

$$\pi_{ajk} = \beta_{a0k}, \text{ for a = 1 to 9}$$

$$\beta_{00k} = \gamma_{000} + \gamma_{001}(TREATEDk) + u_{00k}$$
$$\beta_{01k} = \gamma_{010} + \gamma_{011}(TREATEDk) + u_{01k}$$
$$\beta_{02k} = \gamma_{020} + \gamma_{021}(TREATEDk) + u_{02k}$$
$$\beta_{03k} = \gamma_{030} + \gamma_{031}(TREATEDk) + u_{03k}$$
$$\beta_{04k} = \gamma_{040} + \gamma_{041}(TREATEDk) + u_{04k}$$
$$\beta_{05k} = \gamma_{050}$$
$$\beta_{a0k} = \gamma_{a00}, \text{ for a =1 to 9}$$

Table C.13 lists the number of intervention high schools that have data for the estimation of various trend estimates. For example, the high schools that have gone through intervention more recently have data for only one year after the intervention. Thus it provides information for the estimation of STERM (the short-term trend) and not for the estimation of the medium and long-term trends. All schools contributed toward the estimation of the TREND estimate, as data on years prior to information is available for all schools.

TABLE C.13
Number of treatment high schools with available data to estimate growth parameters

Growth Parameter	Number of Schools
TREND	14
STERM	14
MTREND (at least two years after intervention)	12
LTREND (at least five years after intervention)	5

Tables C.14 and C.15 show the different estimation steps until the final models described in the foregoing were estimated for absences and on-track to graduate rates.

TABLE C.14

Estimates for absences; different models and different propensity score matching methods

	Nearest Neighbor						Caliper	Propensity Weighting
	No Student Covariates; Only u_{00k} Included	No Student Covariates; $u0_{0k}$ and u_{01k} Included	No Student Covariates; u_{00k}, u_{01k}, and u_{02k} Included	No Student Covariates; u_{00k}, u_{01k}, u_{02k}, and u_{03k} Included	No Student Covariates; Full Model	With Student Covariates; Full Model	With Student Covariates; Full Model	With Student Covariates; Full Model
Intercept	0.466***	0.474***	0.473***	0.470***	0.472***	0.475***	0.488***	0.485***
Treated Difference	-0.027	-0.028	-0.020	-0.017	-0.018	-0.035	0.007	-0.047
Pre-Intervention TREND	0.003	0.005	0.004	0.003	0.002	0.030	0.017	0.062
Treated Difference	-0.034	-0.035	-0.034	-0.033	-0.032	-0.029	0.045	-0.037
First Year of Intervention (STERM)	0.057	0.075	0.089	0.092	0.096	0.066	0.194	-0.069
Treated Difference	**-0.233**	**-0.251**	**-0.277**	**-0.288**	**-0.292**	**-0.298-**	**-0.292-**	**-0.217**
Trend in First Four Years (MTREND)	-0.074	-0.057	-0.046	-0.054	-0.059	-0.049	-0.049	-0.007
Treated Difference	**0.053**	**0.057**	**0.057**	**0.076**	**0.081**	**0.077**	**-0.076**	**0.033**
Later Trend (LTREND)	0.139	0.130	0.121	0.117	0.134	0.228*	0.128	-0.012
Treated Difference	-0.139	-0.066	-0.082	0.116	-0.048	-0.141	-0.065	0.062
Announcement Year	0.106	0.104	0.103	0.103	0.103	0.065	0.065	-0.017
Grade 10	0.031	0.031	0.031	0.031	0.031	0.152***	0.091***	0.157***
Grade 11	-0.020	-0.020	-0.020	-0.020	-0.020	0.136***	0.069***	0.130***
Grade 12	-0.064***	-0.064***	-0.064***	-0.064***	-0.064***	0.116***	0.037***	0.123***
Prior Reading Score						-0.081***	-0.081***	-0.089***
Male Student						0.067***	0.067***	0.063*
White Student						0.054	0095*	0.188
Asian American Student						-0.227-	-0.371**	-0.118
Latino Student						-0.179***	-0.047***	-0.007
Student With IEP						0.034**	0.035***	0.057
Student Old for Grade						0.297***	0.302***	0.286***
Neighborhood Concentration of Poverty						0.055***	0.056***	0.072***
Neighborhood Social Status						-0.015*	-0.007	-0.020
Variance Components								
e_{ijk}	0.87872	0.87872	0.87195	0.87872	0.87872	0.81530	0.79462	0.80494
r_{0jk}	0.08127***	0.05608***	0.04148***	0.02692***	0.02539***	0.02696***	0.02639***	0.02515***
u_{00k}	0.05837***	0.05875***	0.06146***	0.06329***	0.06346***	0.06726***	0.05186***	0.04111***
u_{01k}		0.02014***	0.00583*	0.00863*	0.00917*	0.00676-	0.00709	0.00372
u_{02k}			0.10205***	0.08214***	0.08321-	0.07175	0.05275	0.07474-
u_{03k}				0.00934***	0.01498***	0.01412***	0.02311***	0.02422***
u_{04k}					0.01109*	0.01277*	0.04036	0.01709***
Number of Observations								
Students	180,092	180,092	180,092	180,092	180,092	151,285	83,259	749,897
Schools	14 Treated, 10 Control	14 Treated, 10 Control	14 Treated, 10 Control	14 Treated, 10 Control	14 Treated, 10 Control	14 Treated, 10 Control	6 Treated, 7 Control	14 Treated, 60 Control

Note: Significance: $-p < 0.10$, $*p < 0.05$, $**p < 0.01$, and $***p < 0.001$

TABLE C.15

Estimates for on-track to graduate; different models and different propensity score matching methods

	Nearest Neighbor						Caliper	Propensity Weighting
	No Student Covariates; Only u_{00k} Included	No Student Covariates; $u0_{0k}$ and u_{01k} Included	No Student Covariates; u_{00k}, u_{01k}, and u_{02k} Included	No Student Covariates; u_{00k}, u_{01k}, u_{02k}, and u_{03k} Included	No Student Covariates; Full Model	With Student Covariates; Full Model	With Student Covariates; Full Model	With Student Covariates; Full Model
Intercept	-0.125	-0.125	-0.123	-0.123	-0.123	-0.081	-0.110	-0.099
Treated Difference	-0.082	-0.082	-0.092	-0.089	-0.090	-0.076	-0.046	-0.059
Pre-Intervention TREND	0.084	0.083	0.084	0.083	0.084	0.078	0.061	-0.017
Treated Difference	-0.035	-0.034	-0.036	-0.035	-0.036	-0.030	-0.028	0.008
First Year of Intervention (STERM)	0.273	0.271	0.265	0.254	0.257	0.248	0.378*	0.439
Treated Difference	0.089	0.089	0.090	0.096	0.096	0.070	0.112	0.014
Trend in First Four Years (MTREND)	0.084	0.084	0.083	0.097	0.087	0.071	0.023	0.035
Treated Difference	0.011	0.014	0.015	0.017	0.020	0.029	0.073	0.067
Later Trend (LTREND)	-0.160	-0.161	-0.161	-0.162	-0.1617	-0.127	-0.104	-0.046
Treated Difference	0.014	0.016	0.039	0.069	0.054	0.050	0.229	-0.030
Announcement Year	0.006	0.006	0.012	0.011	0.012	0.000	-0.043	0.202
Prior Reading Score						0.368***	0.344***	0.363***
Male Student						-0.592***	-0.547***	-0.620***
White Student						-0.308*	-0.330-	-0.626
Asian American Student						0.905	0.685	0.748
Latino Student						0.323***	0.427***	0.092
Student With IEP						0.243***	0.245***	0.232
Student Old for Grade						-0.045	-0.068*	-0.036
Neighborhood Concentration of Poverty						-0.093**	-0.078**	-0.124
Neighborhood Social Status						0.013	0.012	0.015
Variance Components								
e_{ijk}	0.99854	0.99586	0.899598	0.99603	0.99601	0.99436	0.99700	0.99624
r_{0jk}	0.08477***	0.08166***	0.05980***	0.06187***	0.05980***	0.07139***	0.03646***	0.07569***
u_{00k}	0.06191***	0.06207***	0.05843***	0.05763***	0.05958***	0.07560***	0.02107**	0.08165***
u_{01k}		0.00254-	0.00457	0.00414	0.00330	0.00329	0.00279	0.00284
u_{02k}			0.17088***	0.09195*	0.10215	0.07541	0.04632-	0.13890
u_{03k}				0.00637	0.00210	0.00289	0.00553-	0.00423
u_{04k}					0.00370	0.00501	0.00193	0.00829
Number of Observations								
Students	49,851	49,851	49,851	49,851	49,851	43,591	23,188	209,066
Schools	14 Treated, 10 Control	14 Treated, 10 Control	14 Treated, 10 Control	14 Treated, 10 Control	14 Treated, 10 Control	14 Treated, 10 Control	6 Treated, 7 Control	14 Treated, 60 Control

Note: Significance: -$p < 0.10$, *$p < 0.05$, **$p < 0.01$, and ***$p < 0.001$

Endnotes

Executive Summary

1. These four models are turnaround model, restart model, school closure model, and transformational model. State Race to the Top Fund: Final Rule (2009).
2. This office was previously known as the Office of School Turnaround. AUSL is a local school management organization charged with the training of teachers to affect whole-school transformation; it partnered with CPS to transform low-performing schools.
3. de la Torre and Gwynne (2009).
4. Because CPS did not consistently administer tests to the same grade levels over the period being studied, we were unable to examine changes in test performance at the high school level. A student who is on-track to graduate by the end of ninth grade has enough credits to move on to tenth grade and has no more than one semester F. Students on-track to graduate at the end of ninth grade are three and a half times as likely to graduate in four years as students who are off track. See Allensworth and Easton (2005 and 2007).
5. Herman, Dawson, Dee, Greene, Maynard, Redding, and Darwin (2008).
6. Bryk, Bender Sebring, Allensworth, Luppescu, and Easton (2010).
7. Luppescu, Allensworth, Moore, de la Torre, and Murphy, with Jagesic (2011).

Introduction

8. See Meyers and Murphy (2008); and Wolk (1998).
9. These four models are turnaround model, restart model, school closure model, and transformation model. State Race to the Top Fund: Final Rule (2009).
10. U.S. Department of Education (2010).
11. Picucci, Brownson, Kahlet, and Sobel (2002); Rhim, Kowal, Hassel, and Hassel (2007); Murphy and Meyers (2008); Kowal and Hassel (2005); Herman, et al. (2008); Calkins, Guenther, Belfiore, and Lash (2007); Charles A. Dana Center (2001).
12. Race to the Top Fund: Final Rule (2009).
13. A student who is on-track to graduate by the end of ninth grade has enough credits to move on to tenth grade and has no more than one semester F. Students on-track to graduate at the end of ninth grade are three and a half times as likely to graduate in four years as students who are off-track. See Allensworth and Easton (2005 and 2007).

Chapter 1

14. Wong (2000), p. 100.
15. de la Torre and Gwynne (2009).
16. See box on federal models of reform.
17. Hess (2003).
18. Finnigan and O'Day (2003).
19. CPS (1999).
20. A few more schools have been closed for low performance in Chicago but were not included in the study. The reason is because either no other school reopened in the space or the new school did not serve similar grades. For a list of these schools, see Appendix A.
21. de la Torre and Gwynne (2009).
22. Charter schools are independently operated public schools that are not subject to the same state laws, district initiatives, and board policies as traditional public schools. Charters are operated pursuant to Illinois Charter Law. Charter school teachers are employees of the nonprofit governing board or education management organization hired by the nonprofit board.

    Contract schools are independently operated public schools under Renaissance 2010. Contract schools operate pursuant to the Illinois School Code, are managed by an independent nonprofit organization, and employ teachers who work for the nonprofit. Contract schools have an advisory body composed of parents, community members, and staff.

    Performance schools are operated by CPS and employ CPS teachers and staff. These schools are subject to the collective bargaining agreement between CPS and the Chicago Teachers Union and other labor organizations. They have flexibility, however, on many areas (e.g., curriculum, school schedule, and budget). In lieu of Local School Councils (LSC), Performance schools have an alternative local school council, which allows parents, community members, and staff to be involved in all aspects of the school's activities.
23. Renaissance 2010 initiative was launched in 2004 as "an initiative designed to create more high quality educational options across Chicago." Any new school opened in Chicago since 2005 has been labeled a "Ren10" school. Chicago Public Schools (2010a).
24. Partnership for Leaders in Education (2010).
25. Flavia Hernandez, personal communication, March 19, 2010; Adrian Willis, personal communication, March 23, 2010.

26 Public Impact (2008).

27 Bridget Altenburg, personal communication, March 27, 2010; Christina Fradelos, personal communication, March 27, 2010.

28 For a list of donors, see http://www.ausl-chicago.org/support-donors.html.

29 CPS (2009a).

30 CPS (2009b).

31 For a detailed account of the Performance Policy, see http://www.cps.edu/Performance/Pages/PerformancePolicy.aspx.

32 de la Torre and Gwynne (2009).

33 These schools include: Flower Career Academy, Orr, South Shore, Bowen, and DuSable, as part of CHSRI; and such other schools as Austin and Calumet.

34 Kahne, Sporte, and de la Torre, with Easton (2006); and Sporte and de la Torre (2010).

Chapter 2

35 Even though schools served fewer students per grade after intervention, there is not enough information to determine whether this translated into smaller class sizes. Schools in the Reconstitution model likely saw a decrease in enrollment, in part, because of a policy enacted by CPS in 1997 that required low-performing eighth graders to pass minimum scores on reading and math tests before advancing to high school. This reduced the number of students eligible to start ninth grade in 1997.

36 Data on distance traveled to school for students in the Reconstitution schools were not available prior to intervention.

37 One of the schools under the Closure and Restart model served only male students; therefore, there was an increase in the male population of 40.4 percent.

Chapter 3

38 Information on hiring from the Reconstitution process comes from Hess (2003). Information on AUSL comes from the AUSL website. Information on hiring for OSI comes from personal communication with the director of OSI.

39 Schools under Reconstitution had only the summer to go through the hiring process in their schools.

40 Illinois teachers are required to have one of four main certificates: early childhood education, elementary education, secondary education, or special education. Teachers without these required certifications were counted as having a provisional certification.

Chapter 4

41 Since the reading and math test scores were standardized to have a mean of zero by grade and year, zero represents the system average in every year (see Figures 8 and 9).

42 Since absences were standardized to have a mean of zero by grade and year, zero represents the system average in every year (see Figure 12).

Chapter 5

43 Research at CCSR has shown that the statistics available to the public (e.g., the percent of students meeting benchmarks) are not good metrics for gauging school improvement. Furthermore the ISAT test itself has been questioned in terms of its equivalence over time, and a change in tests given to students in Illinois also makes it difficult to gauge improvements over time. For details, see Luppescu et al. (2011).

44 Bryk et al. (2010) show larger improvements in school climate and parental involvement in small schools undergoing reform, compared to schools that are large or average in size. See Cotton (1996) and Gladden (1998) for evidence suggesting better student outcomes in small schools.

45 Johnson et al. (2004).

46 Luppescu et al. (2011).

47 Bryk, et al. (2010).

48 Gold, Norton, Good, and Levin, (2012).

49 Herman, et al. (2008).

50 Villavicencio and Grayman (2012).

51 Bryk, et al. (2010).

52 Luppescu, et al. (2011).

Appendices

53 CCSR has a long-standing data sharing agreement with CPS that allows it to maintain an archive of more than 15 years of data on CPS students and schools, with unique student and school identifiers. The archive contains complete administrative records for each student for each semester since 1991, course transcripts of high school students since 1992, elementary and high school achievement test scores of students since 1990, and teacher and principal personnel files since 1994.

54 Haviland, Hagin, and Rosenbaum (2007) for details on group-based trajectory analysis.

55 The logit of the propensity score does a better job differentiating among observations in the extreme ends of the distribution than the untransformed propensity score.

56 This particular width and number of matches per treated unit is described as optimal in Austin (2011).

57 See Morgan and Harding (2006).

58 See Raudenbush (2009).

59 A student who is on-track to graduate by the end of ninth grade has enough credits to move on to tenth grade and has no more than one semester F. Students on-track to graduate at the end of ninth grade are three and a half times as likely to graduate in four years as students who are off-track.

Notes From Boxes

A State Race to the Top Fund: Final Rule (2009).

B A student who is on-track has accumulated five credits and has no more than one semester F by the end of ninth grade. A student who is on-track at the end of ninth grade is three and a half times more likely to graduate in four years than a student who is off-track.

C See Luppescu, Allensworth, Moore, de la Torre, and Murphy with Jagesic (2011).

ABOUT THE AUTHORS

MARISA DE LA TORRE is an Associate Director at CCSR. Her work involves studying different Chicago Public Schools' policies, including high school choice and school closings. Her work on high school choice in Chicago was recently published in School Choice and School Improvement. Currently, she is studying a number of different reforms aimed at low-performing schools and indicators of high school readiness. Before joining CCSR, she worked for the CPS Office of Research, Evaluation, and Accountability. She received a master's degree in Economics from Northwestern University.

ELAINE ALLENSWORTH is Interim Executive Director at CCSR. She is best known for her research on early indicators of high school graduation, college readiness, and the transition from middle to high school. Her work on early indicators of high school graduation has been adopted for tracking systems used in Chicago and other districts across the country, and is the basis for a tool developed by the National High School Center. She is one of the authors of the book Organizing Schools for Improvement: Lessons from Chicago, which provides a detailed analysis of school practices and community conditions that promote school improvement. Currently, she is working on several studies of high school curriculum funded by the Institute of Education Sciences at the U.S. Department of Education and the National Science Foundation. She recently began a study of middle grade predictors of college readiness, funded by the Bill and Melinda Gates Foundation. Dr. Allensworth holds a Ph.D. in Sociology and an M.A. in Urban Studies from Michigan State University. She was once a high school Spanish and science teacher.

SANJA JAGESIC is a Research Assistant at CCSR. She holds an M.A. in Sociology from the University of Chicago and a B.A. in Sociology and German from Wellesley College. She is currently working toward her Ph.D. in Sociology at the University of Chicago.

JAMES SEBASTIAN is a Senior Researcher at CCSR. His research interests include school organization, organizational theory and behavior, and urban school reform. He received his M.S and Ph.D. in Educational Leadership and Policy Analysis from the University of Wisconsin Madison.

MICHAEL SALMONOWICZ is a doctoral candidate at the University of Virginia's Curry School of Education and a former Research Analyst at CCSR. He was a CPS teacher for three years. He received his B.A. in English from the University of Michigan.

COBY MEYERS is a researcher at the American Institutes for Research. His research interests include school turnaround, school effectiveness, urban education, and program evaluation. He plays integral roles in various school turnaround initiatives—an area in which he has presented and published, including coauthoring the book Turning Around Failing Schools: Lessons from the Organizational Sciences. He received his M.A. in secondary education from the University of Kentucky and his Ph.D. in education leadership, policy, and organizations at Vanderbilt University.

DEAN GERDEMAN is a Principal Researcher on the Education, Human Development, and the Workforce team at the American Institutes for Research. Gerdeman leads and supports federally sponsored education research, evaluation, and technical assistance projects. He is deputy director of the Regional Educational Laboratory Midwest, a $45 million research center funded by the Institute of Education Sciences to serve a seven-state region, overseeing multiple project teams in applied education research and analysis. Gerdeman serves as project director for a $2 million Department of Education "Investing in Innovation" evaluation of a nationally recognized teacher certification initiative. Previously, Gerdeman was a program officer in the Institute of Education Sciences, where he managed a $105 million program portfolio. He is a past recipient of the American Association for the Advancement of Science policy fellowship at the NSF, in which he consulted with agency officials on evaluation and management of graduate education programs. At the University of California, Los Angeles (UCLA), he served as a researcher in science education and a field supervisor for first-year science teachers in urban schools. Gerdeman earned a doctorate in education and master's degrees in biology and education from UCLA.

This report reflects the interpretation of the authors. Although CCSR's Steering Committee provided technical advice, no formal endorsement by these individuals, organizations, or the full Consortium should be assumed.

UCHICAGOCCSR

CONSORTIUM ON CHICAGO SCHOOL RESEARCH

Directors

ELAINE M. ALLENSWORTH
Interim Executive Director
Consortium on Chicago
School Research

JENNY NAGAOKA
Deputy Director
Consortium on Chicago
School Research

MELISSA RODERICK
*Hermon Dunlap Smith
Professor*
School of Social Service
Administration
University of Chicago

PENNY BENDER SEBRING
Founding Director
Consortium on Chicago
School Research

Steering Committee

RUANDA GARTH MCCULLOUGH
Co-Chair
Loyola University

MATTHEW STAGNER
Co-Chair
Chapin Hall Center
for Children

Institutional Members

CLARICE BERRY
Chicago Principals and
Administrators Association

JENNIFER CHEATHAM
Chicago Public Schools

CHRISTOPHER KOCH
Illinois State Board of
Education

KAREN G.J. LEWIS
Chicago Teachers Union

Individual Members

VERONICA ANDERSON
Communications Consultant

ANDREW BROY
Illinois Network of
Charter Schools

AMIE GREER
Vaughn Occupational
High School-CPS

RAQUEL FARMER-HINTON
University of Wisconsin,
Milwaukee

REYNA HERNANDEZ
Illinois State Board of
Education

TIMOTHY KNOWLES
Urban Education Institute

DENNIS LACEWELL
Urban Prep Charter Academy
for Young Men

LILA LEFF
Umoja Student Development
Corporation

PETER MARTINEZ
University of Illinois
at Chicago

GREGORY MICHIE
Concordia University
of Chicago

LISA SCRUGGS
Jenner and Block

LUIS R. SORIA
Ellen Mitchell
Elementary School

BRIAN SPITTLE
DePaul University

KATHLEEN ST. LOUIS
Project Exploration

AMY TREADWELL
Chicago New Teacher Center

ARIE J. VAN DER PLOEG
American Institutes for
Research

JOSIE YANGUAS
Illinois Resource Center

KIM ZALENT
Business and Professional
People for the Public Interest